MW01046094

Data-driven model for social-ecommerce integration

By

Balvinder

LIST OF FIGURES

LIST OF TABLES

LIST OF ABBREVIATIONS AND SYMBOLS USED

B2B	**Business to Business**
B2C	**Business to Consumer**
C2B	**Consumer to Business**
C2C	**Consumer to Consumer**
E-commerce	**Electronic Commerce**
JSON	**Java Script Object Notation**
OSN	**Online Social Network**
SNM	**Social Network Mining**
XML	**eXtensible Markup Language**
URL	**Uniform Resource Locator**

TABLE OF CONTENTS

CONTENTS	PAGE NO.

ABSTRACT

Since the inception of internet, Online Social Network (OSN) and E-commerce websites have emerged as the main gateway. On the e-commerce websites people buy/sell products or services by making monetary transactions through online payment system like debit card, credit card, UPI, payment wallet, internet banking. By 2021, e-commerce sale is expected to cross $4.5 trillion worldwide. At the same time online social networking websites like Facebook, Twitter, Instagram etc. have attracted billions of people to spend time on these platforms. People remain active on online social networks for information sharing, personal activities sharing, product reviews, sentiment expression, opinion expression, picture sharing, advertising their product or service etc.

To exploit the scope of billions of people for product promotion and selling, online social Network websites like Facebook is providing business page tool. E-commerce companies can create business page on Facebook and invite people to like page. This helps them to build audience for business page. Facebook allows companies to share their product's images, videos, content in the form of posts where page audience can like a post, share post to their network or comment on the post which may be the review of product / service, may be expression of their sentiment, may be complaint about the product, sharing of their knowledge about the product or tag post to a friend who may need it or recommend a friend.

This data provided by the audience on business page can be analyzed by the company by data mining techniques and can be useful for the company for product promotion, product improvements if any or for any type of decision making. e.g. let x be mobile manufacturing company which sells mobile phones online and through its business page it posts and promotes any phone. After using the phone consumer can like the product, provide good or bad review in comment section, write a complaint, or recommend a product via sharing that post. All these activities can by analyzed through insight section, which can be useful information for company. This integration of OSN and E-commerce can exploit the market for its benefit.

In the present research work, a design of a working model on integration of OSN & E-commerce is proposed. This model basically extracts unstructured data provided by the Facebook business page audience in the comment section as an expression of their views, reviews, sentiment in the form of text. By a wrapper program it converts the unstructured data into structured data on five categories, which is explained in the present research work. These reviews from the comment section is extracted by using Facebook Graph API tool in JSON format, which is then converted to XML standard format using the Python language. The extracted reviews in the string format is passed to the list of individual words. These individual words list is filtered to extract useful words. Then from these useful words pattern is generated by classification in bad, satisfactory, good, and excellent and complaining category. A graph is generated for a post for these categories and representation is made on number of bad, satisfactory, good, excellent and complaining categories. A graph for percentage analysis is also generated for comment reviews. These patterns generated from reviews can be analyzed by company for product/service promotion, products improvement etc.

The study has aimed at following research objectives

1) To study and evaluate the existing models relating to e-Commerce and Online Social Network;
2) To extract different patterns of data from e-Commerce and Online Social Network pages;
3) To propose a model to represent relationship between e-Commerce and Online Social Network;
4) To compare the proposed model with existing models.

The proposed model consists of four phases 1) Business Account Setup and Audience Building Module. 2) Reviews Data Extraction Module. 3) Intelligent Review Selection and Pattern Generation Module. 4) Pattern Analysis and Visualization.

Business Account Setup and Audience Building Module have four sub modules 1) OSN Account Sign up: 2) Business Page Creation 3) Setup and load data on Business Page via post 4) Building Audience to Generate Traffic on Business Page.

This module is basically a setup module. All the account login setup, business page setup, creating posts and building page audience are covered in this module. This module also generates the reviews from the end users on a business post in the form of unstructured textual data.

Reviews Data Extraction Module have four sub module 1) Login to Facebook Graph API Module by Authentication 2) Getting Access Token for your Facebook Business Page 3) Extraction of Data using Graph API's Nodes, Edges & Fields 4) Conversion of JSON data into XML format.

Thus module uses the data generated from the first module in the comment section. By passing through an authentication process and using Facebook Graph API explorer tool it extract the data into .json format. This json file is finally converted into XML file, a standard format widely accepted on the internet.

Intelligent Review Selection and Pattern Generation Module have six sub modules 1) Input Reviews into String: 2) Cleaning of String 3) Convert Reviews String into List of Individual words 4) Extraction of Useful Words & Categorization 5) Generation of no. of Words from Predefined Set 6) Pattern Generation

This module focuses on the pattern generation from the data extracted in XML format. Data generated in XML format is converted into string data type. The string is then split into a list of individual words and stored into List data type. To extract the useful words only, list is filtered by eliminating the stop words. After eliminating the stop words, string list of useful words is put into comparing process to generate bad, satisfying, good excellent, complaining or none category words. All words in the list is compared with a predefined set of synonym words. From all the review comments, an overall pattern is generated to tell that how many users have given bad, satisfying, good or excellent category comments. It also generates the complaining comments, so that the company can see how many users is complaining online on social media.

Pattern Analysis and Visualization have two sub modules 1) Pattern Analysis 2) Pattern Visualization by Graph

This module focuses on the Pattern analysis. Data is generated in different categories and percent analysis method is used to analyze the patterns. To view the data in visualization form bar charts are generated in frequency and percentage. As these patterns have uncovered the hidden patterns by data mining, these patterns can help the companies in product improvement or any type of decision making.

So finally a 15 steps, four phased model is designed which attract unstructured data from the online social network's users and by using the wrapper it convert this data into structured data with hidden patterns generated. It also draw the pattern graph for visualization.

At the end of thesis the proposed model is compared with the existing model to draw the difference and similarities between them.

CHAPTER 1
INTRODUCTION

Since the inception of internet, Online Social Network (OSN) and E-commerce websites have emerged as the main gateway. On the e-commerce websites people buy/sell products or services by making monetary transactions through online payment system like debit card, credit card, UPI, payment wallet, internet banking. By 2021, E-commerce sale is expected to cross $4.5 trillion worldwide.

At the same time online social networking websites like Facebook, Twitter, Instagram etc. have attracted billions of people to spend time on these platforms. People remain active on online social network for information sharing, personal activities sharing, product reviews, sentiment expression, opinion expression, picture sharing, advertising their product or service etc.

To cash these billions of people available on the online social networking website, e-commerce companies and social networking websites can join the hands. Today, online social networking websites are providing a platform to the businesses to promote their products or services to these social media users. Online Social Networking websites not only provides e-commerce companies a due platform, but they also provide insights data, which shows how people behave after seeing their ads and many more. This integration of OSN and e-commerce is the main area of the present research work.

The present chapter has been divided into five sections. Section 1.1 provides the introduction to e-commerce, online social networks, data mining and integration of OSN with e-commerce. Section 1.2 discusses about the application of area of OSN & e-commerce. Section 1.3 discusses the need of study for the present research work. Section 1.4 describes the objectives of the present research study. Section 1.5 puts light on the structure of the thesis. These sections have been discussed in detail as below:

1.1 INTRODUCTION

E-commerce [48] is known as buying or selling of products or services over electronic system such as Internet and other computer network. E-commerce companies like Snapdeal, Make my Trip, Amazon, moneycontrol etc. are experiencing exponential growth in these days. Today, with the easy availability of Internet on smart phones and Personal Digital Assistant devices, one can easily access E-commerce websites, users can explore various products and services on their smart phones or PDA devices. Users can buy any product or service according to their own choice. Products or Services are available at their door step which saves users' time and money.

In India with the huge success of cash on delivery option ecommerce companies has generated the faith among the customers through various platforms like e-commerce, OSN, integrated view of e-commerce and data mining. These have been further elaborated in following sub sections.

1.1.1 ONLINE SOCIAL NETWORK (OSN)

Online social networks are the new ways to communicate, collaborate and contribute one's knowledge on the internet via OSNs platforms like Facebook, Twitter, LinkedIn, Instagram etc. In the short time span Facebook has witnessed a large number of registered users. People around the world can have 24x7 online presence and can share any type of personal or commercial information on their network and reach to the others. These OSNs encourages users to build online mesh of relationships. Companies are also reaching out to the people to provide awareness about their product or service through online social networking sites like Facebook.

OSN websites have become tools for connecting people with each other on the internet and it reflects the activities of their social life. Facebook is the leading OSN website with 2.2 billion active users as of (January 2018). (Source: - en.m.wikipedia.org/wiki/Facebook). Every 60 seconds 5,10,000 comments are posted on Facebook and 2,93,000 statuses are uploaded and 1,36,000 photos are uploaded (Source

2

Social Skinny),with this type of data being uploaded , Facebook is one of the challenging computer application artifacts.

On the OSN websites people disseminate information, post, personal activities, review products, share pictures online, give product reviews, express their opinion and sentiments and can share all type of text, audio & video contents. Online social networking websites like Facebook etc. are engaging users on the real time to share their opinion or reviews for a particular post. Analysis of these reviews, opinion is a fascinating topic for the business organizations. Data on the OSN websites are usually structured and unstructured [89] in nature. Most of people now express their sentiments/opinions on the social media e.g. if people do not like the service or product of any company , they share views about the product or services immediately on the social media & companies now take this activity very seriously as it may damage their reputation on internet. So we can say online social media is making an impact on the society. There are a number of famous social media platforms available on the Internet few are Facebook, Twitter, LinkedIn, Instagram, Pinterest, Google + etc.

1.1.2 E-COMMERCE (ELECTRONIC COMMERCE)

E-Commerce is defined as the process of buying, selling, transferring, or exchanging products, services or information via the public Internet or private network [141]. Buying and selling of goods or services involve activities [1] like monetary transaction, e-CRM (Customer Relationship Management), e-cash management, delivery system etc. Now these days' people on the Internet can buy any product or service through websites or specific apps on android or IOS. Few famous e-commerce websites are amazon.in, amazon.com, flipkart.com, snapdeal.com etc. which provide interactive user interface using shopping cart concept to facilitate the users for easy buying. Big companies like Amazon, Paytm , Flipkart etc., are providing cash back into their money wallet to encourage the users for buying online.

3

E-Commerce companies have integrated various e-payment systems [36] like payment through debit card, credit card, e-wallet, UPI, internet banking or cash on delivery options also available in India.

With the coming of big companies in the field of e-commerce, business organizations are now able to establish a trust factor in the mind of Consumers. Brock [22] presented the framework of trust in e-commerce, where consumer's first choice to buy the product is through trusted partners only. E-commerce websites have addressed the security issues [8] like authentication, electronic signature, and commercial sales in the electronic environment. With the advancement in the technology e-commerce websites have covered the authentication issues by means of user ID-password login with One Time Password linked with consumer's mobile number for safe transaction. So today e-commerce companies are successfully implementing challenges like security issues, trust issues, e-payment issues and privacy issues [21]. They are also handling risk factor in e-commerce [44]. Thus, by [110] companies implement two approaches for e-commerce so that consumer should adopt e-commerce. First approach is technology centered which covers user interface features, content & design, usability, ability to effectively dialogue with consumers and security measures.

Another approach is consumer centric which covers product perceptions, service quality, trust, shopping experience etc.

In these days big e-commerce players have designed & developed advance websites & apps which provide world class shopping experience to the consumer and companies are also working on quality factor also, which is a major issue these days. A partial list of online e-commerce websites is given below:

flipkart.com, jbong.com, snapdeal.com, myntra.com, amazon.in, naaptol.com, ebay.in, yebhi.com, flickr.com, yepme.com, groupon.co.in, infibeam.com, dpauls.com, homeshop18.com, makmytrip.com, 99acre.com, alibaba.com, zovi.com, olx.in, tradus.in etc.

4

1.1.3 DATA MINING

The process of extracting useful and meaningful information from the data [2] is known as the Data Mining. Few activities of the data mining are classification, clustering, association rule mining, sequencing and forecasting related to data.

➢ Classification is concerned with the decision making process extracted from data.
➢ Clustering is the process of partitioning the data records in to clusters (groups) that share similar properties.
➢ Association rule mining is concerned with discovery of relationship between data attributes.
➢ Sequence mining is the process of determining the relationship between data attributes according to temporal ordering or some other ordering.
➢ Forecasting is process of predicting the future by analyzing & sequencing of data.

Social Networking Mining [2] is the mining of data being uploaded on the online social network websites, which includes photos, text, reviews, opinion, sentiments etc. has attracted Data Mining Community to generate knowledge from this data. The Data generated from this OSN can be used to generate patterns for classification, clustering, trending mining, frequency pattern mining, or prediction model for forecasting etc.

Social networking techniques can be utilized to generate knowledge concerning the social behaviors of users on online environments. In the present research [6,27] social networking mining will be used to extract the data from the reviews [28] from a page & generate the patterns to predict the behaviors of user online environment.

The whole process can be classified [103] as:

➢ **Exploratory data Analysis**—Searching without knowledge of what is being searched and then analysis of data for forecast/prediction
➢ **Descriptive Modeling**---it describes all the data.

5

> **Predictive Modeling** – predicting value of one variable from another known variable.

> **Discovering Rules and Pattern**s—discovering new/hidden patterns

1.1.4 INTEGRATION OF ONLINE SOCIAL NETWORK WITH E-COMMERCE

The term web2.0 [93], collaborative technology, which includes social networks, web services, pod casts, blogs, video sharing, information sharing, RSS feeds, wikis, mesh ups, P2P networking etc. are participative tools where users are allowed to interact with each other. Few Applications of Web2.0 are as below:

> Web2.0 in education
> Web2.0 in Academic Library
> Web2.0 in Geographic Information System(GIS)
> Web2.0 in e-banking
> Web2.0 in e-commerce.

The term "Enterprise 2.0" which state to focus only on those platforms that the companies can buy or build in order to make visible the practices and output of their knowledge workers.

The two Independent terms can be combined to generate an effective result for the companies. Jacques Bughin discussed about the rise of enterprise 2.0 where he explained how the people in an enterprise are using the web2.0 tools like web services, P2P marketing, collective intelligence, social networks, Pod casts, Blogs, RSS feeds, wikis and mesh ups and average awareness of web2.0 technology is 66% and Investment into at least one web2.0 technology is 75% .

This gives the platform to integrate online Social Networking with e-commerce, where OSN websites like Facebook, LinkedIn etc. can be utilized to perform e-commerce activities. Lai [86] presented the concept of social commerce where he put the concept of integration of e-commerce in social media.

6

Thus, integrating online social networks with E-Commerce can be a profitable experience for companies as explained by [127] on the basis of CBR approach (Case Based Reasoning) where they analyzed that two friends on social network follow online similar purchasing behaviors.

Not much research has been done on this topic and online social networking websites like Facebook, Twitter etc. are trying to en cash the traffic on OSN via e-commerce, where they can aware the customers about the products and encourage them to buy online. Facebook, online social networking website provide companies to create business pages, buy & sell groups, give access to market place to perform e-commerce activities.

1.2 APPLICATIONS OF E-COMMERCE AND OSN

This study is based on the data collected from the reviews by the customers. This study may have a substantial an impact on many ecommerce businesses like

- ➤ Tour and Travel Industry;
- ➤ Online Shopping Industry;
- ➤ Hotel Industry;
- ➤ Online Air Ticket Booking;
- ➤ Online Movies Industry;
- ➤ Restaurant / Food chain industry;
- ➤ Education Sector. etc.

1.3 NEED OF STUDY

These days, every business Firm is promoting their business online through social media networks like Facebook, Twitter, Instagram etc. Taking an example of Facebook where business firm can create pages to promote their business online. Business firms promote their product or services by posting banners, text, videos on such pages.

7

Customers, like business firm Page(s) and after using their product or service customer gives review about their experience regarding product /service. This has been exemplified in the figure no 1.1 given below:

Figure 1.1: Facebook Business Page (Source: facebook.com)

As these reviews are given in the comment section and other customers before buying the same company product/service read these reviews from other customers and these reviews can affect the buying of company's product/service by the other customers who are planning to buy the product.

As this is unstructured data, written in the any language like English, up to now not much research has been done. These reviews, if analyzed effectively can give proper insights to the customers and if the company is providing good service then company may earn huge profits from these reviews, but at the same time if the company is providing bad service then the customer can save their money from these companies.

So need of the study arises from these reviews, which surely affect the business of ecommerce companies. Hence due understanding of needs and gaps in existing studies, the study has focused upon following research objectives.

8

1.4 Objectives of Present Study

The Study has aimed at following research objectives:

- ➤ To study and evaluate the existing models relating to e-Commerce and Online Social Network.
- ➤ To extract different patterns of data from e-Commerce and Online Social Network pages.
- ➤ To propose a model to represent relationship between e-Commerce and Online Social Network.
- ➤ To compare the proposed model with existing models.

Keeping in mind above objectives, the study has adopted a particular structure of research, mention as below.

1.5   STRUCTURE OF THESIS

The thesis is being structured in the form of seven chapters. Brief description of each chapter is given below.

Chapter 1 deals with the Introduction to the concepts of Online Social Networks, E-Commerce, Data Mining and integration of OSN with E-commerce.

Chapter 2 emphasizes upon the work of eminent researchers and provides detailed review of the literature in the field of OSN and E-commerce and integration of OSN and e-commerce. It explored data mining techniques in OSN and E-commerce. It also explores the persistent challenges which still need to be addressed in OSN field.

Chapter 3 focuses on the research methodology adopted to carry out the present research work.

Chapter 4 focuses upon data extraction tools by Facebook, the famous Online Social Network through Facebook Graph APIs. It also describes the steps to generate the pattern of data using data mining techniques.

Chapter 5 presents the proposed work i.e. OSN-ECOM Model to Integrate Online Social Network and E-commerce which can be further used by the companies to assess their performance of product / services on the OSN business pages which may affect the sale of their product / service.

It also evaluates the performance of all modules individually as well as the OSN-ECOM Model in its entirety. Existing literature has been explored to retrieve the existing models for analysing and comparing the proposed model with existing models.

Chapter 6: A Comparison of proposed model has been made with already existing models.

Chapter 7 presents the conclusions and the main contributions of this research work along with the scope of future work.

Summary

This chapter has provided a brief introduction about Online Social Networks, e-Commerce, Data Mining Concepts and integration of OSN & e-Commerce. It discusses the application areas and need of study. At the end, it presents structure of the thesis with a brief introduction to each chapter.

CHAPTER 2
LITERATURE REVIEW

Review of literature plays an important and crucial role in research work. It is a document which gives us a comprehensive review of a particular topic. It holds the information about past and present developments.

This chapter describes the work of eminent researchers along with the future scope. The chapter has been divided into 9 sections. Section 2.1 describes the introduction. Section 2.2 presents related literature on the topic of Online Social Network models and its features. Section 2.3 presents the related literature on the topic of E-commerce Models. 2.4 represents the related work on integration of OSN and E-commerce. Section 2.5 presents the evaluation of OSN models. Section 2.6 presents the evaluation of E-commerce models. Section 2.7 presents the evaluation of integration and its future impact on the current research work. All the OSN and e-commerce models are tabulated with study concepts and evaluation under section 2.8. Section 2.9 presents a summary of this chapter.

2.1 Introduction

The rise in the popularity of online social networks websites like Facebook, LinkedIn, Instagram etc. has influenced the consumer's purchasing behaviour in fundamental way. Now a days, online social networking websites users can share any product or service information [84]. These OSN users are also encouraged to show their like or dislike towards the product or services [87]. Online social network consumers may also "consult social community to seek advice in their purchasing decision" [85]. These OSN communities have the potential to influence buying decision of larger social media communities [4]. This integrated platforms allow online users to participate actively in the marketing and target market places and communities to sell products and services [126, 91, 112]. The integration of OSN and E-Commerce is emerging phenomenon for marketers, businesses and researchers alike [8].

11

To be successful on these integrated platforms, user participation is very important factor [7, 16]. There are two types of participations from the users 1) Active Participation 2) Passive participation [155, 156, 158, 25, 94, 119]. Active user participants comment on posts, share the posts, and contribute to the content promotion within the network, while passive users just explore or browse the posts content and does not contribute in content or relationship building [29]. Users on these platforms participate by the motives of Self Interest or on the basis of organisational commitment [16, 29, 158, 25].The community members' have psychological bonds with product or services of any company and if they find such posts on OSN and E-Commerce platforms they show their commitment and participate actively on these posts.

There are three types of Commitment, [1] as defined by Liang, (1) Need based Commitment (2) Affect based Commitment (3) Obligation based Commitment. When user actively participates on OSN-ecommerce integrated platform they contribute to the Content Creation and Content Transmission [29].They actively participate by participation in comment section. Online users also show their commitment on cultural aspects [158] and encourage others to participate. Investigation factor also influence purchasing intention on OSN and E-Commerce platforms. As defined by [7, 17, 156, 114, 12, 55, 76, 122, 128], there are two more factors which influence the purchasing behaviour on OSN and E-Commerce platforms (1) Person Interactivity (2) Machine Interactivity and [29, 114, 148] confirms the effect of users generated on the Conversion rate.

The other factors that influence the purchasing behaviour are listed below as defined by various researchers:

i. E-wom [9, 3, 46] Community user's rating, reviews and recommendation influence the Sales and Revenues.

ii. No. of likes, no. of positive evaluations affect the Conversion rate.[148]

iii. Advertisement also influence [83] the Click through rate and significantly impact Performance and Sales.

iv.   Customer's Interaction on the OSN, loyalty has impact [49, 54, 153, 139, 30] on the new product adoption.

v.   Close friends have more impact than the weak ties on the purchasing decision [148].

vi.   Demonstrate [49] that it may be Strong tie or weak tie, they have an impact on influencing the purchase decision.

Thus, we can summarize that Review of Literature shows that customer method, participation, trust, machine and person interactivity, Active participation influences the customer's purchase decision on the OSN-Ecommerce platforms. User's Interaction and participation is the key component in influencing the user's purchasing decision. This can be better understand by OSN models described in section 2.2.

2.2 Online Social Network Models

In this section, we shall discuss about the Online Social Networks (OSN) and its models. OSNs are platforms [100] on the internet which connect people with each other to share their views, photos, content etc. few applications of OSNs are information sharing, personal activities posting, product reviews, online picture sharing, opinion expression, sentiment analysis advertising etc.

A Social Network can be defined as a Graph G= (V,E) , where V is the set of vertices which represents the nodes in the network and E is set of edges with which all the nodes in the network are connected. For the real world nodes represent the individuals in the network and edge represents the social relationship between the individuals.

With the various researches on Social Networking, OSN models were developed after analyzing the characteristics of real life social network and these characteristics are:

- ➢ Random Graph;
- ➢ 'Small World' Property;
- ➢ Scale Free State;
- ➢ Local Transitivity.

13

The above Characteristics has been explained as jbelow:

Random Graph Theory: With this theory, the construction of a graph happens by adding the edges between the n isolated vertices. The probability of adding an edge is same for all the vertices. Erdos-Renyi Model explained in the coming section is based on this theory.

Small World Property: A Network constructed with "small-world" theory is represented as a graph in which most of the nodes in a graph are not neighbors of each other, but neighbor of any one can become neighbors of each other by reaching with a small number of steps/nodes.

The diameter l which reflects the "small-world" property can be presented as

$$l \alpha Log(|V|)$$

Where |V| is cardinality of V.

Scale Free State: A network model which follows the power law in degree distribution is known as scale free network. Degree Distribution in power law for the real large network can be represented as:

$$p(k) \sim k^{-\gamma}$$

Where γ is a parameter whose values range is between 2< γ<3.

Local Transitivity: It represents the property that on social network if X is friend of Y , and Y is friend of Z, then there is chances that X is also friend of Z.

$$X \rightarrow Y, Y \rightarrow Z \text{ then } X \rightarrow Z$$

Depending upon above characteristics now we shall discuss about the OSN models.

2.2.1 Online Social Network Characteristics

Characteristics discussed above of random graph, small-world, scale free distribution and local transitivity have been applied to the models of Social networks rigorously. In this research study four modeling paradigm are used

> ➤ Random Graphs

➢ Small-world

➢ Power law

➢ Local Transitivity.

Erdos-Renyi model was developed using the random graph theory and widely used in several empirical studies. Watts-Strogatz Model was developed using the small-world property. Similarly Barabasi-Albert Model and Iterative Local Transitivity Model was developed using the scale free distribution and local transitivity model respectively. Study of all models is discussed in coming sections.

2.2.2   Erdos-Renyi Model

This model is based upon the random graph theory [38, 39] defined in 1959. Erdos and Renyi has defined two models viz. Randomize Node Pair model and Randomize Edge Present / absent model.

Model 1: Randomize Node Pair Model also known as G (n,m) model where graph is based on the basis of two parameter n and m.

- n = the number of nodes in a graph.
- m = the number of edges in a graph.

In this model a graph is started by picking a pair of nodes at random among the n nodes and insert an edge between them if it is not present. Edges are being added until exact m edges have been added to complete the graph.

Model 2: (Randomize Edge Present/Absent model)

It is G(n,p) model with two parameters n and p.

- n is the number of nodes and
- p is the probability that an edge is present between two nodes.

If there are n numbers of nodes then possible number of edges will be $\frac{n(n-1)}{2}$ in the network.

15

In this model probability of having a connection is defined by p factor. P is between 0 and 1.

If p is higher, connections are higher, and if p is low then connections are low. Average node degree for this model is defined by p (n-1).

Degree of a node in undirected graph is defined by the number of edges connected to the node as an end vertex. In this model, probability of a given node has degree k is defined by the binomial distribution:

$$\binom{n-1}{k} p^k (1-p)^{n-1-k}$$

In this model binomial distribution approximations are based on the value of n and is defined as

Table 2.1: Degree Distribution for Erdos-Renyi Model

for small p	Binomial distribution	$\binom{n-1}{k} p^k (1-p)^{n-1-k}$
For large n	Poisson Distribution	$\frac{\mu^k e^{-\mu}}{k!}$ where $\mu = p(n-1)$
For normal n	Gaussian Distribution	$\frac{1}{\sigma\sqrt{2\pi}} e^{-\frac{(k-\mu)^2}{2\sigma^2}}$

When we compare this model with real world it is a poor predictor of degree distribution. This model results in poisson distribution that exponential decay, whereas the real world exhibit power law degree distribution that decays much slower than exponential.

Clustering coefficient: Clustering coefficient of a node is the probability that two randomly selected nodes to be edged are already edged. According to Watts & Satrogatz [149] clustering coefficient when applied to a single node is a measure of how complete the neighborhood of a node is.

In Erdos-Renyi Model [38], presence of an edge between two nodes is measured with probability p. when we compare Erdos-Renyi Model with real world on clustering coefficient; it is poor predictor for clustering coefficient. When the network is too small and close to edge density then it can give result on clustering coefficient.

Edge density of a network is known as the actual number of edges in proportion to the maximum possible number of edges.

Density of graph:

$$\delta = \frac{2m}{n(n-1)} = \frac{2pn(n-1)/2}{n(n-1)} = p$$

2.2.3   Watts-Strogatz Model

This model is based on the property of small world effect. In real life like human being friends network, Internet, neurons etc. follows the six degree of separation which is known as small world effect phenomenon [99]. It is observed [99] that typical distance between nodes is small even if the network grows very large.

The Watts-Strogatz Model [149] is based on the two graph properties viz.

➢ Path Length L(p)

➢ Clustering Coefficient C(p).

L(p): It is the measure of separation between the two nodes in a graph.

C(p): It is the measure of associativity with neighborhood, a local property in a graph.

This model has three parameters:

➢ Number of Nodes

➢ Link/Node

➢ Probability, a chance of connecting random pair of nodes for each link in the graph.

For n>>k>>ln(n)>>1, where k>>ln(n) connected graph, Watts and Strogatz found that L~ n/2.k>>1 and C~3/4 as p→0 and L ~ L_{random} ~L_n (n)/ln(k) and C~ C_{random} ~ k/n <<1 as p→1. Thus the regular lattice at p=0 is highly clustered, large world where L grows linearly with n, whereas the random network at p=1, is poorly clustered, small world [102] where L grows only logarithmically with n. Figure 2.1 depicts this concept.

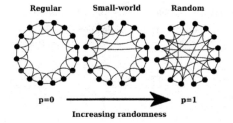

Figure 2.1: Rewiring of regular lattice for Random and Small world by Watts and Strogatz. (Source: Collective dynamics of 'small world' network [149].)

2.2.4 Barabasi-Albert Model

Both the Erdos-Renyi Model and Watts-Strogatz Model works with the fixed number of nodes, that are then randomly connected from Erdos-Renyi Model or reconnected without modifying the N. but in real life networks expand continuously by addition of new nodes and new nodes attach preferentially to other nodes that are already well connected. Thus Barabasi-Albert Model is based on the scale free distributions [77], which indicates that development of large networks is governed [19 ,61] by robust self-organizing phenomena that go beyond the particulars of the individual network.

Barabasi-Albert Model is based on the two main ingredients of self-organization of network in scale free network

  ➢ Growth: Number of nodes in network increases with time.
  ➢ Preferential attachment: it refers to the fact the new nodes tend to connect to nodes with large degree.

This model indicates two simple mechanisms:

Growth: It is the addition of a new node into the network at each timestamp. If we start with m_0 node then after each node timestamp the Barabasi-Albert Model generates network with

$N = t + m_0$ nodes and $m_0 + mt$ links.

18

Preferential attachment: The new node prefers to link to the more connected nodes. The probability $\prod(k_t)$ that a link of new node connects to node i depends on the degree k_i as

$$\prod(k_i) = \frac{k}{\Sigma kj}$$

Preferential attachment is a probabilistic mechanism. A new node is free to connect to any node in the network, whether it is a hub, or has a single link. If a new node has a choice between degree two and degree four nodes, it is as likely that it connects to the degree four nodes.

Degree Distribution given by the Barabasi-Albert Model follows power law distribution and is defined by

$$p(k) = 2m^{1/\beta}\ k^{-\gamma}$$

With $\qquad \gamma = \frac{1}{\beta} + 1 = 3$

Clustering coefficient of Barabasi Albert model is

$$(C) \sim \frac{(lnN)^2}{N}$$

The network diameter, representing the maximum distance in the Barabasi-Albert network, follows for m >1 and large N

$$(d) \sim \frac{ln\ N}{lnlnN}$$

2.2.5   ILT Model (Iterated Local transitivity Model)

The ILT Model is Iterated Local Transitivity Model. This model is based on the property of transitivity which states that if A is friend of b, B is friend of C, and then A is Friend of C.

The ILT Model [127] generates finite, simple, undirected graph (G_t : t≥0) time stamp t, for t>= 1 ; is defined to be transition between G_{t-1} and G_t. With the initial graph G_0 which is any fixed finite connected graph, at a fixed t>=0 , the graph G_t has been constructed. To form G_{t+1} for each node x ∈ V(G_t), add it clone x' such that x' is joined to x and all its neighbors at time t.

This model exhibits a denstified power law and defined by volume of G_t.

$$Vol(G_t) = \sum_{x \, \varepsilon \, V \, (G_t)} deg_t \, (x) = 2e_t$$

The clustering coefficient of G_t is defined by

$$C(G_t) = \frac{\sum x \in v \, (G_t)^{c_t(x)}}{n_t}$$

where
$$c_t = \frac{e(x,t)}{\binom{deg_t(x)}{2}}$$

2.3 E-commerce Models

Electronic commerce (E-commerce) is sharing business information, maintaining business relationships, and conducting business transactions by means of telecommunication networks. [145]. Ecommerce is one of the mostly used applications of internet used for buying and selling of the product or service. We can make a payment through online banking, debit card credit card or payment wallet to buy product or service. With advancement of technology people can buy from their mobile phones through the apps.

Today there are number of web portals available like Amazon, Flipkart, Snapdeal etc. which provide wide range of products at discounted price, which saves time and money for the end users.

In India cash on delivery option is widely successful and many companies are operating on Cash on Delivery Model.

Major types of e-commerce Models [4]

- Business to Business (B2B) Model
- Business to Consumer (B2C) Model
- Consumer to consumer (C2C) Model
- Consumer to Business (C2B) Model

20

2.3.1 Business to Business (B2B)

In B2B Model both the entities are business organizations. The transaction takes place at business to business [79] level. The business organization can make wholesale purchase for their use or for selling product on retail. Top items in B2B ecommerce category are electronics, food, papers, office products etc. Block diagram for the Business to Business model is shown in the figure 2.2 below:

Figure 2.2: Business to Business (B2B) ecommerce Model.

2.3.2   Business to Consumer (B2C)

In B2C ecommerce model business organisation sell their product or service to consumer via Internet for their own use. B2C model is growing in the field of travel services, online Banking, online health services etc. Block diagram for the Business to Consumer model is shown in the figure 2.3 below:

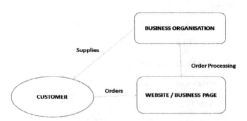

Figure 2.3: Business to Consumer (B2C) ecommerce Model.

21

2.3.3　Consumer to Consumer (C2C)

In C2C model product or services are sold through classifies or auction system. It Classifies system like olx.in, where consumer can sell their product or service to another consumer via a website/app platform. Block diagram for the Consumer to Consumer model is shown in the figure 2.4 below:

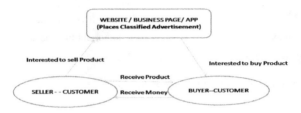

Figure 2.4: Consumer to consumer (C2C) ecommerce Model.

2.3.4 Consumer to Business (C2B)

This model is also called demand collection model. In C2B model, a consumer provides a business with a free based opportunity to market a product or service on consumer's website such as blog. In this model, the website owner is paid to review the product or service through blog posts, videos or audio podcasts. Here consumer creates a value for the business by review.

It is also named as auction model where consumer auction for the product on the business website and website collects the demand bids and then offers the bids to participating sellers. Block diagram for the Consumer to Business model is shown in the figure 2.5 below

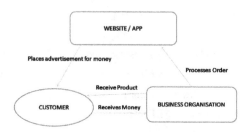

Figure 2.5: Consumer to Business (C2B) ecommerce Model.

After studying these models, it is also quite important to understand integration of OSNs and E-commerce which has been discussed in following sub-section.

2.4 INTEGRATION OF OSN AND E-COMMERCE

After discussing the models of OSN and E-commerce, in this section this section discusses about the integration of OSN with E-commerce. A CBR (Case Based Reasoning) approach [127] on integrating OSN with ecommerce states that two persons with similar interests have   similar purchasing behavior.

$$\text{If } f_1 \sim f_2 \text{ then } ob_1 \sim ob_2$$

where f_1 and f_2 are friends on online social networks and ob_1 and ob_2 are their purchasing behavior on OSN respectively.

Architecture proposed by Zhaohao [157] is shown in Figure 2.6 below:

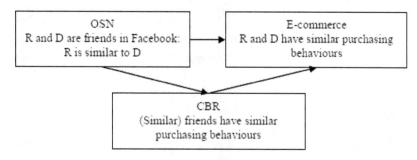

Figure 2.6: CBR architecture for integrating OSN with e-commerce. (Source: [127].)

On the online social networks there are different types of communities [101, 115] like transaction-oriented online communities, interest-oriented online communities, relationship-oriented online communities, and fantasy-based online communities. Out of these categories aim of transaction –oriented online communities is to bring the seller and buyer together and focus on transaction need; where the members get business transaction information [123]. These types of communities [106] on OSN are related with ecommerce activities, which facilitate users for transaction.

Facebook, an online social Networking website, offers business organization to create Business page(s), Marketplace, buy and sell group(s) which integrates social media with e-Commerce. In the similar fashion other networks like Instagram, Pinterest, LinkedIn etc. are on the same line to integrate OSN with E-Commerce to capture online market and encourage the users to buy online or perform transaction.

2.5 EVALUATION OF ONLINE SOCIAL NETWORK MODELS

2.5.1 Evaluation of Erdos Reyni Model

It is developed using the random graph theory where a node added to graph with an edge to any node ad random with probability p. in real world like on www various website are being added on daily basis. World Wide Web, Metabolic Network, Paper Citation Distribution are the application of erdos reyni model.

My evaluation on the application of Erdos Renyi Model on Social network is that when a person creates a new account on the Online Social Network then the account makes connection with another account at random graph theory. On daily basis number of new accounts are being created and growing using the Erdos-Ryeni model.

2.5.2 Evaluation of Wattz strogatz Model

It works on the principle of small word. In the real world people tend to group together in a cluster and want to remain in cluster for other activities. People want to connect to the people who are known to them in some or the other way. For the small world six

24

degree separation rule is applied. One person is known to another person up to six level in the social network.

On the online Social Network profile accounts, pages, groups exists where people with a common interest are attached with each other by creating a cluster known as community. In community they have same type of behavior or interest.

2.5.3   Evaluation of Barabasi-Albert Model

On the online social Network people always get attached to known network according to their preference or interests. As all networks small or big tend to grow with time so scale free attachment is there with preferential attachment.

On OSN profile account, page or Group it grows with time and people join with each other according to their preference.

2.5.4   Evaluation of Iterative Local Transitivity Model

According to this Model transitivity rule is applied in online social network also. This rule says if A is friend of B on OSN and B is Friend of C on OSN then there is probability that A is also friend of C on OSN.

Facebook works on FOF friend of friend model, which is the application of transitivity model. It plays an important role in the growth of any network on the Online Social Network. Using this technique Facebook sends suggestion to the existing accounts to grow using FOF (Friend of Friend) model.

2.6   Evaluation of e-commerce models

E-commerce website works on the B2B, B2C, C2C and C2B model. Amazon, flipkart, snapdeal.com etc. like website works on B2C model to reach to consumer directly. olx.in type of website connects consumer with another consumer. Naukri.com type of website comes under C2B category model, where the consumer generates Business for any Company. Last is B2B where two business connects via website.

2.7   Evaluation of Integration of OSN & E-Commerce

Main point in the evaluation of this model is that, if X and Y are friends on the online social Network like Facebook and if X and Y have similar purchasing habits, then CBR says that similar friends have similar purchasing behavior online.

So this is evaluated that if we combine OSN and e-commerce or if business are allowed to sell on online social network then friends on the social media tend to buy the similar products. This gives opportunities to ecommerce companies to sell their products / service using OSN platforms.

From the above model few queries arises in mind

1. What if two persons are not known to each other on online social network?
2. Can review provided by a person who has experienced product or service online influence the decision of another person?
3. What if a person recommends any product or service to community of people?
4. Are people only following their friends only or do they decide on other factors also?

To find the answers to some of these type of queries present research study worked on the reviews provided by the people online in comment sections on the post of any OSN page. At the end of this chapter all the OSN and e-commerce models has been tabulated with study concepts and evaluation.

2.8   RESULTS AND DISCUSSION

Table 2.2: Concepts and Evaluation of Online Social Network Model

Model Name	Concept	Evaluation
Erdos and Renyi Model	Random Graph Theory	In this model a node can be added randomly and World Wide Web like platforms where websites are being added on daily basis. On such type of platforms it fits better.
Watts-Strogatz Model	Small-world	Most of the social networking sites like Facebook, Twitter, Instagram, linkedin

		etc. are working on the concept of small world where personal profile, groups, pages , marketplace , events etc. are the example of this.
Barabasi-Albert Model	Scale free state with growth and preferential attachment	This model explained about the scale free addition of nodes in the Social network, where network grows with time and they are added to network with preferential attachment. In OSN the network with more number of members attract another member to be added with his choice.
Iterated Local transitivity Model	Local Transitivity	This model explained the concept of transitivity, in OSN this is also true because if A is friend of B, and B is friend if C, then chances are there that A is friend of C. Facebook like application which works on the friend of friend model is implementation of this concept .
Business to Business Model(B2B)	Both the entities are business	This type of model is used for making transaction between the two business houses online e.g. Company distributor or franchisee ordering products or services directly from company through online website.
Business to Consumer Model (B2C)	First entity is business and second is consumer	In this model business house or website is selling their product online directly to consumer. Like Amazon, Flipkart etc.

Consumer to Consumer (C2C)	Both the entities are consumers	In this model, the consumer is selling their product to the other consumer through online website. e.g. olx, droom, quicker etc.
Consumer to Business (C2B)	First entity is consumer and second is business	In this type of model consumer is available for services for business houses like naukry.com,
Integration of OSN with E-Commerce	Case Based reasoning (CBR) approach	This model integrates OSN with e-commerce on the basis of case based reasoning which states that if x and y are friends on the online social networks then they have the similar purchasing behavior. The website like Facebook has integrated business through pages, buy & sell groups, Marketplace feature to encourage the customers to buy through these tools.

Summary

This Chapter has presented an overview of work related to Online Social Network Models, E-Commerce Models and Integrated OSN and E-commerce Model. It presented the study and evaluation of various OSN models like Erdos-Reyni Model, Watts-Strogatz Model, Barabasi-Albert Model, and Iterated Local transitivity Model. It presented the study and evaluation e-Commerce models like Business to Business Model (B2B), Business to Consumer Model (B2C), Consumer to Consumer (C2C), and Consumer to Business (C2B). It also presented the study and evaluation of CBR based OSN & E-Commerce integration model. At the end OSN and e-commerce models were tabulated with study concepts and evaluation.

CHAPTER 3: RESEARCH METHODOLOGY

3.1   Introduction

Methodology describes the process on how this research study has been conducted in order to achieve the objectives. It represents the detailed procedure, tools and techniques adopted to achieve the objectives. It provides blueprint to achieve the goals. It provides the insights into preparing the study design, collection of data from the resources for study, tools and techniques used and data analysis techniques.

The process is shown in the figure 3.1 below which represents the study frame:

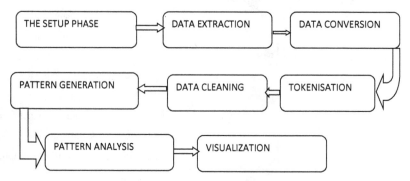

Figure 3.1: Process Diagram for Research Study Framework

The overall methodology starts with the Setup Phase where Facebook business page is created and all the settings are done to generate the data on the page from the page audience. After the data generation, data from reviews provided by the users is extracted and converted into standard format like XML.

Data available in .xml file is stored in the string and with tokenization technique, it generates the individual words. The list of individual words is put into data cleaning to generate the useful words.

The patterns has been generated from the words by the categorization technique and then with percentage analysis and visualization patterns were presented in graphical way. This overall methodology has been used in the coming chapters to achieve the objectives of current study.

This chapter describes the research methodology followed in the present research work. This chapter has been divided into 7 sections. Section 3.1 describes the introduction. Section 3.2 presents the objectives and related questions to present research work. Section 3.3 focuses on the Facebook business page setup, audience building by organizes and paid promotions and page insights options. Section 3.4 describes the data extraction techniques from business page and storage into database. Section 3.5 discusses the various approaches to data analysis. Section 3.6 presents the tools used to carry out the experimentation in the present research work. Section 3.5 presents the summary of this chapter.

3.2   Objectives and Research Questions

The reactions provided by the users in the form of likes and shares are in the form of structured data and comments are in the form of unstructured data. To analyze the structured data various tools are available and provided by the OSN websites. But opinion provided by the page audience in comment section arises few questions whose answers are hidden.

As opinion provided by the online users are influencing the other users on the internet in their decision for buying the product or services. So research questions are

1. How opinions are influencing the decision in purchasing on e-commerce website?
2. How unstructured data can be converted into structured data?
3. How to integrate OSN & e-commerce to build audience on OSN to attract people to give their opinion?
4. How to generate patterns from reviews and visualize them graphically?
5. How to extract the reviews data from Business Page at one go if large number of reviews are available?
6. Which tools will be used to extract data and generate patterns?

30

To get answers to these questions, objectives have been framed on the basis of above research queries, following research objectives have been framed:

- ➢ To study and evaluate the existing models relating to e-Commerce and Online Social Network.
- ➢ To extract different patterns of data from e-Commerce and Online Social Network pages.
- ➢ To propose a model to represent relationship between e-Commerce and Online Social Network.
- ➢ To compare the proposed model with existing models.

To achieve these objectives, a design of study, techniques for data extraction and pattern generation has been described which will be covered in the coming sections. Now we shall see the study design in the coming section.

3.2.1 Research Design

Design of study represents the steps involved in achieving the goals and objective. To achieve the objectives, present research study is dived into four phases:

1. **Setup Phase**: As per the title of research, study integration of OSN and E-commerce is required. This phase of the study covers the setup of an ecommerce company on the online social network like Facebook. This phase covers the detailed designing on creating business page, settings of page, audience building techniques etc.

2. **Data Analysis Phase:** This section focuses upon the primary data extraction and conversion into the standard format like XML. This phase work with the data provided by the page audience in the comment section. As this is first hand data, it is considered as primary data. On the business page data provided by the users in the comment section is considered as their opinion for a particular product or

service. A wrapper program / algorithm will be written for the extraction of data and conversion of data from an OSN business page.

3. **Pattern Generation Phase**: This section generates the patterns from the unstructured data, provided by the users as their opinions. This section discusses the techniques of storing reviews into string, cleaning of string, tokenization technique for generating words from string, categorization of words to generate patterns. Visualization of patterns play an important role in decision making. This section also discusses the bar charts visualization method with color code on different categories for better presentation and understanding.

4. **Tools**: As tools play an important role in the research study. This section discusses about the tools used to complete the study. In the present study, Graph API Explorer has been used to extract data and python language is used to generate the patterns and generate the bar charts as demanded by the present study.

Following research methodology has been used.

3.3   The Setup Phase

The main aim of the e-commerce companies is to reach to millions of users available on the online social networking websites. Companies can aware, generate interest or sell their products to these online users. To aware users about their product companies need a platform where they can promote products on social networks. For achieving this goal online social networking websites like Facebook, Instagram, LinkedIn etc. provide business page tool, where companies can create & setup their page and reach to audience by applying different techniques. Next section 3.1.1 describes and introduces the business page set and audience building.

3.3.1   Business Page Set up and Audience Building

To integrate online social network with e-commerce and to view its impact [43, 60], e-commerce companies need a platform on social media websites. Through this OSN

32

platform companies can promote their product or service to online users. OSN websites like Facebook provide business page tool on which companies can create posts in the form of text, images or videos to promote their products or services.

Before reaching to the millions of online social networking users, a company should create and setup a business page properly. Company should provide proper description about the page, setup logo and appropriate cover photo, setup Call-to-Action button, location, and timings of business. So that online users should understand about the company's page and like it. In the coming sections details about the OSN websites, business page setup, audience building and insights will be discussed.

3.3.1.1 Online Social Network Websites

Online Social Network websites are the convenient ways for the online users to stay connected with friends and website members. These websites have low cost and are easy to interface to interact with each other. Online Social Networking websites allow users to publish and control content easily. These website users can share content, images, videos, opinion, sentiments, etc. with just a click of a button. These OSN websites also provide media entertainment services, job search, event creation, shopping facility etc. to attract the more number of users on their platform. Now I shall discuss about few online Social Network websites in the coming section.

FACEBOOK

Established in 2004 [80], Facebook is famous online social networking website with more than 2.3 million active users at the end of 2018. [source:statista.com/statistics/264810/number-of-monthly-active-facebook-users-worldwide/.]

Facebook allows individuals to create profile on their websites. Users can share text, image, videos, upload their profile picture and cover photo, comment on the post(s), share friends post on their wall, chat with their friends, tag their friends, can give like, love, ha-ha, wow, sad or angry reactions on the post[31]. Facebook implements the graph

33

network properties of random graph theory proposed by Erdos & Renyi [38, 39], small world property given by wattz- strogatz[149] and scale free state with growth and preferential attachment by barasasi-albert[15]. Users can grow their network with friends, interact in a small group or attach to celebrities or companies through their page. Apart from the waste features, Ivan Di Capua [24] has identified six categories for which Facebook is utilized by users. These are

1. Maintaining relationships
2. Learning about others
3. Recognition
4. Communication
5. Social influence
6. Experience

With the ever changing nature and addition of features by Facebook, it has become a strong online social network for interaction.

INSTAGRAM

Established in Oct 2010 with url instagram.com, Instagram has 1000 million or 1 billion active users as on January 2019. [source:statista.com/statistics/272014global-social-network-ranked-by-number-of-users]

Instagram was acquired by Facebook in 2012[IN1]. Instagram is free photo and video sharing online social networking website. With 95 million posts and 500 million stories per day [source: blog-hootsuite.com/instagram-statistics].

Instagram ranked 6th in the world in social networking sites [source:statista.com/statistics/272014global-social-network-ranked-by-number-of-users].

Other Websites

Apart from Facebook and instagram as discussed above YouTube, Whatsapp, Wechat, Reddit, Twitter, Sina weibo, Tik Tok, Qzone, QQ, Douban, LinkedIn, Baidutieba, Skype,

Snapchat, Pinterest and line are famous online social network platform with millions of users, where users interact with each other online.

3.3.1.2   Facebook Business Page

To promote the business on social networks, Facebook provides tool, known as page [FB6] through this companies can create their own customized page and share their vital information about their product or service. By promoting their product and other information companies can create own brand image, using page companies can target specific audience and communicate with the users [26].

Facebook allows users to set profile picture like company logo and cover photo which can depict about the company's service through image. To encourage the users to take action, when user visit a page, Facebook provides Call-To-Action CTA button facility, with which company can set one button out of various options available like shop, book, contact, download app, learn more about business or join community. Facebook page provides publishing tools, inside, setting, hosting events, ads center etc. option to facilities the companies for better communication with the page audience.

Companies can have page ratings, give feedback and message directly to customer options through page.so, Facebook page is a very useful tool which can be utilized by e-commerce companies to mark their presence on online social network.

3.3.1.3   Facebook Post

To aware the page audience about their product or service companies can post their content via Facebook page post. Facebook provides options to create post(s) where companies can post text content, photo, video, feeling activity, checking location, write notes, create poll, give list, create watch party, get messages etc..

Apart from this a company can go live, create event, create any offer or create job through post. Post is a powerful way to reach to the way page visitors, engage them, encourage visitors to share post for viral marketing [26] and the user can provide review or feedback in comment section. The content provided by the page audience in comment section can be used for the opinion mining [28], which can identify sentiment, feedback about product, emotions or review about the product or service.

3.3.1.4   Business Page Audience Building

After setting up Facebook business page, next step is to build the page audience who regularly visits the page to know about product or service offered by the company. Facebook users can like [75] any page of their choice in which they have interest and follow the page to get notifications whenever company updates page or posts. To build the audience for Page Company can promote page by paid online advertisement [47]. Through the personal profile company can invite friends on the Facebook to like their page. There are two types of traffic visitor on the business page.

1. Organic traffic
2. Paid traffic

Organic traffic is the number of visitors that visit page without paying or through search result. Paid traffic is number of visitors that visit a business page by paying to online social networking websites like Facebook. Cost per click, cost per mile [FB7] and fixed amount for space on page are the famous paid advertisement options online. Cost per click, is the amount that the advertiser pays to OSN site to get click on Ad from a user matching the target audience. Cost per mile is amount paid by advertiser to OSN for giving one thousand impressions to target audience.

By offering these paid ads as sponsored ads company can encourage interested Facebook users to like their page and become prospectus for future sale. Amazon India a famous e-commerce company has 10 million likes on their Facebook business page as on Feb 2019. In the similar fashion Snapdeal, MI India, flip kart, Jabong etc. E-commerce platform has millions of followers on the Facebook business page and on other OSN platforms.

36

3.3.1.5   Facebook Ads Options

With the development of internet and advancement in technology, advertising on the internet has become major activity [82]. Companies develop advertising strategies to target internet based users through search engine, email or online social networks. On the online social networking websites, people with one group or friends have shown similar purchasing behavior [127]. OSN websites like Facebook can target the audience by showing them similar ads as purchased by their group or friends. With the success Facebook, LinkedIn, YouTube like platforms advertising on online social networks has received more attention.

Facebook has developed a platform named facebook.com/business, where companies can register and create advertisements. From the business page companies can directly select Boost Post Option to promote any Post on the page to your customized page audience. Facebook provides facility to create targeted audience by age, sex and location. If a company has its own website, by installing Facebook Pixel a Company can target website visitors who have Facebook Account to advertise their product or Service Company can also promote its page, website or business at local level with in few miles through Advertisement.

To run a paid advertisement on Facebook or Instagram or on OSN, companies have to set a goal for running ads campaign. Campaign is an activity performed to run advertisement like post to promote any discount campaign, or any awareness campaign etc. On Facebook there are three types of goal options available.

1. Awareness campaign
2. Consideration campaign
3. Conversion campaign.

Awareness campaign is run to aware about product or services by reaching out to OSN users. Consideration campaign is run by the companies to encourage the users to consider their products before making any buying decision. Lastly conversion campaign is run by companies to encourage customers to take action as required by the companies such as buying product, download app, store visit etc. Facebook runs these advertisements to target customers specifically or broadly as selected by the company.

3.3.1.6   Reactions on page post

When a company posts on the online social network, passive type of users just view the post, they do not react on the post. But active users always like or react to the post. Users can give their reactions in the form of pressing like button of different variations of love, ha-ha, sad, wow etc. as provided by the OSN website. Users can share post in their network online, users can give reviews or opinion in the comment section provided by the OSN websites.

Facebook provides various options to provide reactions on the post(S). Users can press like, love, ha-ha, wow, sad etc. to give their reaction. Users can post emoji [138] to provide their sentiments on any post, or user can share. Company's post in his/her network. These types of reactions are known as click speech [33] which provides reactions through simple clicks.

User can also provide his/her opinion in comment section in textual format, which is a more active form of click speech form [45, 33].

Sentiment through comments can be categorized into positive, negative or network polarity [92]. These comments can be analyzed by the companies to get feedback from the users. Different researches are going on this topic which can analyze the unstructured data and generate patterns, which can be utilized by companies for decision making or forecasting.

By explaining these reactions on Facebook, E-commerce business companies can establish a virtual relationship [140] with Facebook users. This virtual relationship can contribute in sales improvement, brand building and focus on implement in other areas.

38

Thus we can say that reactions provided by the users on Facebook brand page depending upon various factors [67] can be utilized by companies for establishing relationships, brand awareness, consideration, sales conversion and forecasting.

3.3.1.7   Facebook Page Insights

Beauty of the inbound marketing is that, it provides analytics for campaigns run by the companies. When any company runs promotional campaign on Facebook page, it provides analytics for campaign through insights tab section available in business page. It is provided by the URL http://facebook.com/insights.

Facebook Page provides insights about how people are engaging with page. It provides various metrics like post clicks, reactions on post, comments on post, no of post shares, number of people reaches, video views etc. it also provides insights for the posts which have more number of engagements, people's demographic data, organic and paid reach, page's videos, page's followers , page's views and previews, page's recommendations, and number of page likes.

Companies are interested to view the insights on the following factors [96]

1. **Reach**: Reach tells about the number of people who had any posts from company's page enter their screen. These are the passive Facebook page users who just view the post.

2. **Engagement**: It is the customer's behavior [96] towards any brand, firm or page post. Users can click on post, react, comment, shares, view videos etc. are types of engagement. Engagement insight provides data on these above said factors, these are the active Facebook page users who show interest and interact with companies.

3. **Conversion**: Conversion insights provide data about Call-to-Action. For example number of app downloads, number of clicks on link provided, sale conversion, catalogue downloads etc.

As mentioned by the Christou [32], Facebook insights tool is used by all the companies as a standard marketing tool as compared to Google Analytics used by 57%, Hashtag tracers by 43% and Hootsuite by 29%. So we can say that Facebook insights tool is most beneficial tool to draw appropriate results.

Now I shall discuss the various Facebook insights options provided by Business page. It is as follows:

1. **Overview Section**: In the overview section Facebook provides page summary which includes data about actions on page, page views, page previews, page likes, post reach, post engagements, page responsiveness, videos, page followers, recent promotions by page through boost posts. It shows data of yesterday, today, last 7days, last 28 days or as customized by the company according to dates range.

2. **Promotions Tab:** it shows the data insights of recent promotions on the page.

3. **Followers tab**: - Followers tab shows the total page followers as of today, net followers and where your page follows happened.

4. **Like tab**: - It shows the total no. of likes, net likes and where your page likes happened.

5. **Reach Tab**: Post reach tells the number of people who had any posts from company's page enter their screen it shows the post reach and total reach for the page.

6. **Page Views Tab**: - This section shows the data about total people who have viewed your page, and page views by section, by age & gender, by country and by device.

7. **Page Preview Tab**: - This tab shows the total page previews & page previews by age and gender. Difference between page views & page previews is that page views is the no, of times a page's profile has been viewed by login & log out users, whereas page preview is the no. of times people hover over a page picture or a page name to see a preview of page.

8. **Action on Page**: - This tab shows the data insights of actions performed on the page by followers like website clicks, person no. clicks, action button clicks, get

direction clicks. It also shows the no. of people who clicked action button, by age & gender, by country, by city & by device.

9. **Posts tab**: - This tab shows data about the posts like all posts published, average reach, average, engagement, top posts from page and timeline which shows the page fans who are online.

10. **People Tab**: - It shows the data about the people who are page fans, followers and reach to people. Besides this it also shows data about events, stories on page, groups linked to page, videos and messaging insights.

3.3.1.8. User' Opinions

Business Page audience can provide their opinions on a product or service in the comment section of post. These opinions provided by the users are considered as reviews who have experienced the product or service. Opinions are playing very important role on the internet and one of the effective factor for e-commerce companies for sales boost. Till now not even a single OSN website provides the insights about these unstructured reviews and the present study is covering this topic. Opinion mining is the research topic in the coming years with its challenges. The present study will provide the roadmap to the companies to handle reviews on product post in an effective way. All the work from model building to pattern generation and visualization are based on the reviews provided by the page audience.

The present section provided the research methodology about the setup of web pages on online social network website by the e-commerce companies. In the next section data extraction and its methodologies have been discussed.

Section 3.3 have discussed about the Facebook page setup and audience building process in detail. Facebook page insights which provides analytics about the reach and reactions by the people on the business page are also discussed. Insights are very useful for the future action plan. Page Insights only provide the data about structured data like no. of likes, shares, reach etc. but it does not provide insights about the opinion provided by the users in comment section, which is unstructured data. Next section 3.4 provides the data

41

extraction and storage techniques from the comments section, which is the one of the goals of my research.

3.4 Data Extraction Techniques and Process

There are two types of data which is available 1) Primary data 2) Secondary data. Primary Data is the data collected from the end users in the raw form and it is first hand data, whereas secondary data is a type of data which is published by the other authors in journals and second hand data. In the present research study, primary data will be used which will be collected from the Online Social Network Business page audience in the form of opinions or reviews in the comment section of a product post.

As a technical research study, the present study will not collect the data from end user directly. This study will use the data provided by the online users in the comment section, so data extraction has to be implemented to collect and use the data.

Data extraction a process of extracting the data from a post on a business web page of online social network. As discussed in the previous section that e-commerce Company has to first setup the business page and then create a post to get the reviews from online users.

As a company has to post text, images or videos about the product or service on its business page, then page audience will start reacting on the post and will provide likes and reviews in comment sections. On one post there may be hundreds of reviews which will be considered as Primary data for the present study. Now the major challenge is to extract these reviews which will be utilized in pattern generation. Now we shall discuss about the data extraction process and techniques which will be implemented in the present research study.

3.4.1 Data Extraction and Storage

Retrieving the data form the sources like OSN business pages is known as data extraction, Data retrieved can be converted and stored in the data base or data warehouse for further processing.

In the current study, data has been extracted from Facebook business page using a tool provided by the Facebook. The tool is Facebook Graph API explorer Tool. Now we shall discuss about the tool and carry out the data extraction process using this tool.

3.4.1.1 Extraction of Data using graph API explorer

The Graph API Explorer tool can be accessed by login to this tool. API is primary way to get data in and out from the online social networking sites.

Login-Authentication of User

This is the first step and user is asked to login [133] to his account after passing the authentication with user-id and password provided by the account. Only authenticated user has the rights to access the data. The first step to use Facebook graph API explorer is to login into the Facebook system with your personal account. To pass the authentication step Facebook uses Oauth2.0 tool.

Oauth 2.0 Tool

Oauth 2.0 [137] is authorization protocol layer, where an end user, the resource owner can grant an access to his protected data stored at the resource server without sharing his username and password with the third party services. This can be achieved by authenticating user credentials directly with the server trusted by authorization server, which issues the access to data by providing the access token.

Oauth 2.0 has four roles:

1. **Resource owner:** It refers to the end user entity who can grant access to a protected data/ resources.
2. **Resource Server:** the server which is hosting the end user data/resources and the server will issue the access token to third party to access resources owner data / resources.
3. **Client:** this can be an application or program which sends requests on the behalf of the resource owner for accessing protected data with its authorization.
4. **Authorization server:** This is a server that issues access token to the client after authenticating the resource owner.

After passing the authentication process, next step will be getting the access token on the page from which you want to access the data. As only the admin or owner of the page can access the data, one must login accordingly. Now we shall discuss about the access Token

Access Token

Facebook allows users to access Graph APIs by providing an access token. User can get access token by three ways:

1. User Access Token
2. App Access Token
3. Page Access Token

Access token is provided to the user after passing the authentication process. User access token is provided with the data access permission like user data permissions, events, groups, pages, instagram, videos, insights. According to your access token provided user can access the data on Facebook objects.

After getting the user access token, users can now get the page access token on which the users want to perform any operation or extract data.

Graph API Explorer Tool

Facebook Graph API provides http/1.1 for transferring the data and all endpoints require https. To extract the data from Facebook, reading operations begin with node with its unique ID. E.g. A page node with unique ID can be used to receive the data from Facebook Page.

We can use command:

Get https://graph.facebook.com/<pageID> to retrieve the information about the page.

Nodes in the Facebook have edges, which help in returning the collection of other nodes connected with them. To extract the data using edge, user can use node ID and edge name in the path URL. E.g. to read the post nodes on a page /feed edge is used.

Get http://graph.facebook.com/<pageID>/feed

It will retrieve the data in JSON format while extracting the data from Facebook with the nodes and edges you can specify the filters on data. To achieve this fields are used. Fields are node properties. With fields you can specify which field you want to retrieve by using field parameter and listing each field. e.g. to retrieve about me information one can use : *me/?fields=about.* So with the help of the nodes, edges, and fields user can extract the data from Facebook pages in JSON format.

To retrieve the comments from the post on a page we can use: Get https://graph.facebook.com/<pageID_postID>/Comments. This command will extract the comments on a particular post given by users as a feedback or review for the post. After getting the access token on page, following command was executed in the Facebook Graph API explorer: 1444109289155226_2078984755667673/comments, Where 1444109289155226 is page id and 2078984755667673 is post id for a particular post which makes it a complete node and /comments edge to retrieve the comments from a post. Figure 3.2 given below shows the data retrieval from a Facebook page after giving a command.

45

Figure 3.2: Facebook page comments data retrieval.

3.4.1.2   Conversion of Data

Facebook Graph explorer API returns the data in JSON which make it difficult for end user to read the data in proper format and use it for further processing. So, we need to convert the data into XML. XML is Extensible Markup Language and format provided by XML is easy to use, all the web application development languages accept data in XML format which can be formatted with XSL for better presentation.

To convert the JSON data into XML format python will be used. Python is high level object oriented programming language [78]. Python is used for the development of data science program development. Python is free and open source language with large standard library for regular expressions, web browsers, unit testing, email, image manipulation, threading, databases and a lot of other functionality.

Python [124] provides modules and packages which is a collection of python programs used to solve any problem by programming. In this paper we have used xmltodict package to convert JSON code into xml code.

3.4.1.2.1. JSON (Java Script Object Notation)

It is language independent and open standard format to represent and transfer the data object in Attribute-Value pair. JSON represents the data "Name": "Balvinder" format where "Name" is the attribute of the object and "Balvinder" is value for the object. When

46

we will try to extract the data from Facebook Graph API explorer tool it will look like as shown in the Figure 3.3 below for clear understanding:

Figure 3.3: Representation of data in JSON format in Graph API Explorer.

3.4.1.2.2 XML (eXtensible Markup Language)

Extensible Markup Language is a format to store the data which is suitable for human readability and machine readability. It defines the set of rules to store the data in any document. Tags are used to construct the data markup which represents an element in XML. It is used to represent the data structure. XML is data centric and Document centric. Data centric has fixed XML schema, whereas document centric are loosely structure and do not follow XML schema.

Benefits of XML:

1. Extensibility
2. Machine Readable
3. Self-Descriptive
4. Multiple Data Types
5. Fast adoption by Industry

47

6. Standard

7. Openness

8. Simplicity

9. Multilingual

10. One server view for distributed data.

Figure 3.4 given below shows the representation of data in xml format. It stores the data in tags creating a tree structure.

```
C:\python1\output.xml
C:\python1\output.xml
<?xml version="1.0" encoding="UTF-8"?>
- <message>
    <data>
        <created_time>2018-12-10T14:30:02+0000</created_time>
        - <from>
            <name>Balvinder Taneja</name>
            <id>1444109289155226</id>
        </from>
        <message>learn full course</message>
        <id>2078984909000991_2273182602914553</id>
    </data>
    - <data>
        <created_time>2018-02-14T16:48:40+0000</created_time>
        <message>Yes balvinder ji i want to learn</message>
        <id>2078984909000991_2079133982319417</id>
    </data>
    - <data>
        <created_time>2018-03-02T07:31:14+0000</created_time>
        <message>Yes</message>
        <id>2078984909000991_2086959371536878</id>
    </data>
    <paging>
        - <cursors>
            <before>MwZDZD</before>
            <after>MQZDZD</after>
        </cursors>
    </paging>
</message>
```

Figure 3.4: Representation of data in XML format.

The sub sections 3.4.1.2.1 and 3.4.1.2.2 presented JSON and XML. There are few differences and advantages of xml over json which is presented in the table 3.1 below:

Table 3.1: Comparison between XML and JSON

Criteria	XML	JSON
Language	Mark-up Language	It is Format
Data Structure	Tree Structure	Attribute Prefix
Processing	can perform processing	Does not perform processing

48

Transmission Speed	Slow Transmission	Fast Transmission
Size	Big and Bulky	Compact
Array Support	No	Yes
Encoding	UTF-8 , UTF-16	UTF, ASCII
Safety	Safe with DTD	Safe with JSON Parsing

With the so many benefits over the JSON format, XML has been used to store the data in the present research study.

3.4.1.3 Data Storage

The data is extracted and converted to XML format. These generated XML files can be stored in the data ware house. A wrapper program written in python language will be used to process the extracted xml file, so xml files can be stored on the hard disk and a folder for storing the files can be created from where it can be retrieved easily.

3.5 Approaches to Data Analysis

3.5.1 Data mining

The process of discovering patterns or knowledge from a large amount of data is known as data mining. Data mining functionality has four [57] areas:

1. Predictive Analysis
2. Clustering Analysis
3. Frequent Pattern Analysis
4. Outlier Analysis

3.5.1.1 Predictive Analysis

Predictive analysis is divided into classification and regression.

49

Classification: It is supervised learning and prediction is carried out on unknown data. Decision tree, neural network etc. are the classification algorithm.

Regression: Regression is supervised learning and prediction is carried out on the numerical data. Trend analysis, multivariate estimation are examples of regression.

3.5.1.2 Clustering Analysis

It is unsupervised learning where similar objects are grouped together to find the patterns. K-means clustering, hierarchical clustering, fuzzy clustering, density clustering etc. are the examples of cluster analysis algorithm.

3.5.1.3 Frequent Pattern Mining

Taking a set of data, applying statistical method to find the unknown pattern within the predefined data set is known as frequent pattern mining. Basket Data Analysis [104], Cross marketing and selling, medical treatment, catalog design are a few examples of frequent data mining.

3.5.1.4 Outlier Analysis

In the data set, if an object is different and inconsistent, then it is known as outlier. These objects do not comply with general behavior of model and can be noise or exceptions in the data. There are four approaches:

> ➢ Statistical Approach
> ➢ The Density Based Local Outlier Approach
> ➢ Deviation Based Approach
> ➢ Distance Based Approach

In the present research study, Frequent Pattern mining, classification and clustering of data are used to find the patterns from the reviews.

3.5.2 Pattern Visualization

The process of identifying the pattern [152, 111] from data and providing insights is known as data mining. The process of data summarization can be implemented through visualization. As insights provides economic value and competitive advantage to business, data visualization techniques [144] provide direct prediction of pattern generated.

Visualization representation [90] facilitates a better understanding of results. Data visualization techniques uses two steps 1) Exploration of Data 2) Analysis of Data. To present the data in the graphical way different Visualization techniques are available these are 1) Standard Graphs 2) Geometric Techniques 3) Icongraphic Techniques 4) pixel-oriented Techniques 5) Hierarchical Techniques.

In pattern visualization for generating the graphs some common tasks are performed [14,143]

- Correlation
- Clustering identification
- Outlier detection
- Pattern identification
- Visualization graph generation.

Combining the visualization and data mining is also known as visual data mining.

For the current study pattern visualization will be generated with the Bar chart. After the text data passed to wrapper program, using the tokenization and categorization techniques pattern will be generated. Percentages on data will be calculated and then using the python matplotlib graph with color code will be generated for the pattern visualization.

3.6 Tools

3.6.1 Python

Python is an object oriented high level language [18,71] which can be used to write program for Graphical User Interface, system programming, network and internet programming, component integrity, database programming, numerical programming[11] etc.

Python programming language is used by the leading software companies like Google, Youtube, Intel, CISCO, NASA, HP, IBM,NSA, JPMargon, UBS etc. to do Artificial Programming, movie animation, scientific programing etc.

Python has numerous libraries [78] of packages to complete the tasks in robust and within the time frame. To help the researchers to implement code python provide packages for scientific programming. Few of these packages are Numpy, Scipy, SQL Alchemy, Pytables, matplotlib, json, xmltodict, Elementtree etc.

While using a programming python language provides [65] variables, objects, functions, advance data types like lists& sequence, containers, dictionaries, nested data structure support, control & flow statements, comprehensions, libraries, database support, json & xml support, plotting graphs with matplotlib, Numpy package for scientific programming, boids, and testing framework. With all the above mentioned features python makes the programming for research very easy to achieve the desired goal. With above mentioned features and others python is becoming the fastest growing [6] language in the world as analysis given by Stakoverflow and Q &A hub.

With high level language, numerous module, vectorization capabilities, support for scientific computing [23], better performance on serial and parallel scientific computations, python is becoming first choice to solve the research issues.

The present research study will also be using the python with pycharm editor to generate the patterns from data. Xmltodict & json packages will be used to extract and convert the data in xml format. ElementTree package will be used to traverse the xml nodes to retrieve and store the data in String. List data type will be used to store the data, data tokenization and data categorization.

Matplotlib will be used to generate the Bar graphs for visualization. All the algorithms written in python will be presented in the coming chapters.

3.6.2 Facebook Graph API Explorer

Facebook Graph API Explorer [62, 63] is a tool provided by Facebook Company for developers which is used to construct and perform Graph API queries, test queries, access token generation, login permission etc.

The Graph API is http based API [66] which can be used to query data, post new data, images etc. Graph API is composed of nodes, edges and fields. Nodes represents an entity like a page, a user, a comment etc. Edge represents the connection between the two nodes like comments on a post etc. Field represents the info about the entity like date of birth of a user, URL of page etc.

As the present research study works on the data provided on the Facebook business page in the comment section. To extract the data from Facebook business page this Graph API explorer tool will be used. Application Programming Interface [109] will help to retrieve the data using its nodes and edges from the Graph API explorer tool. The present research study will use the page node and comment edge to retrieve all the comments from the business page in one go. Facebook provides this comments data in the JSON format.

3.7 Summary

This chapter covered about the research methodology carried out in the present research study. In the introduction section it presented the study framework with diagram which has shown the various steps involved in the study process. Questions were raised in the research questions section for which answers has been found in the investigation. Objectives of the research study are also presented. Research design is divided into five phases 1) setup phase 2) Data extraction technique and process 3) Approaches to data analysis 4) Pattern Visualization 5) Tools Used.

Setup phase discussed about the OSN websites, business page setup on OSN, Facebook page post, Page audience building, reaction on post, Facebook ads options to attract traffic, Facebook Page insights, and users' opinion in comment section.

Data extraction and process phase covered the data extraction from business page using Graph API Explorer tool and conversion process from json to XML format.

Approaches to data analysis covered the data mining techniques for the pattern generation and visualization techniques.

Tools used section discussed about the python language and Facebook Graph API explorer tools which will be used to implement the experiment in present research study.

CHAPTER 4
DATA EXTRACTION

To carry out the research study, primary data is needed. Primary data is the data which is first hand data provided by the end user. On the Online Social Networking websites large amount of data is being uploaded everyday by the users in the form of text, images , videos, reviews , comments likes etc.

There are two types of data is available on the Online Social networks

1. Structured data
2. Unstructured data

Structured data is available in the form of no. of shares, number of likes on the posts, number of page likes etc. whereas unstructured data is available in the comment section and this is primary data provided by the page audience on the post of a page.

4.1 INFORMATION EXTRACTION FROM ONLINE SOCIAL NETWORK PAGE S / WEB PAGES

This section focuses on the techniques available to extract the data using data mining.

4.1.1 Information Extraction Approaches

For the information extraction Kaiser and Miksh designed learning techniques and knowledge engineering techniques. Sarawafi defined this technique as rule based technique or statistical approach and learning based approach.

In the rule based technique human interaction is essential for the requirement and functions. Statistical method are effective approach for unstructured data extraction in NLP, fact extraction and textual data.

In learning based approach, a system has been developed using regular expressions to perform the extraction of data.

4.1.2 Wrapper Programs

Wrapper is a complete algorithms family that a company executes to extract the information from unstructured data and convert them into structured data for the future processing and decision making. Semi-automatic wrapper technique can also be used with visual extraction technique, regular expression based approach or logic based approach. These techniques are also used to extract the data from web pages or online social network pages.

The specific areas where wrappers techniques are used are Social networks, Social Book Marking, news groups, ecommerce retail websites, comparison website and communities are the famous ones.

The present research study focuses only on the data extraction from the online social networking websites like Facebook. Data extraction also has many applications areas, few of them are enlisted below.

Social applications of Data extraction are:

1. Online Social Networks.
2. Social Bookmarks.
3. Opinion Sharing.
4. Web Harvesting.
5. Comparison e-commerce shopping.

4.2 METHOD OF EXTRACTING DATA

This section focuses on the data extraction method used to extract the data from Facebook business page. The current research study uses the Facebook business page to get the primary data from the end user in the comment section and then extract the data from page using developer tool provided by the Facebook Company.

The tool name is Facebook Graph API explorer tool. Facebook provides graph APIs and graph API explorer [136] to extract [37] the data from owned Facebook pages. User can use Facebook URL https://developers.facebook.com/tools/explorer to extract the data.

Graph API explorer framework is as shown in the Figure 4.1

Figure 4.1: Facebook graph API explorer tool.

(Source: https://developers.facebook.com/tools/explorer)

All the requests are passed to the graph.facebook.com and for videos requests are passed to graph-video.facebook.com

To extract the data from the Facebook Page using Graph API explorer tool 4 steps are used for the process and steps are given below:

1. Login-Authentication of User;
2. Access Token for user/page;
3. Extraction of data using nodes, edges, fields;
4. Conversion of data.

For the better understanding of the process steps a diagram is drawn and shown in Figure 4.2 below:

57

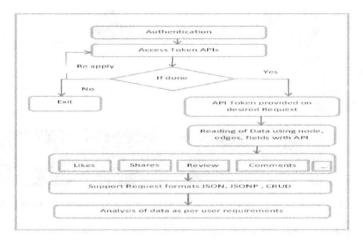

Figure 4.2: To show complete Facebook extraction Process.

Now in the coming section all the steps involved in the data extraction from a Facebook page are discussed in detail.

4.2.1. Login-Authentication of User

This is the first step and user is asked to login [133] to his Facebook personal account after passing the authentication with user-id and password provided by the account. Only an authenticated user has the right to access the data. An Image from developers.facebook.com/tools/explorer has been copied from the Facebook developer website to show the login screen as shown in the figure 4.3 below:

Figure 4.3: To show Login screen of Facebook. (Source: developers.facebook.com/tools/explorer)

The registered user is asked to login into his/her Facebook developer account. After passing through the authentication process the user is taken to the developers account screen as shown in the Figure 4.4 below:

Figure 4.4: Facebook Developers Graph API Screen after login. (Source: developers.facebook.com/tools/explorer)

4.2.2 Access Token

After login into the developers account, the next step is to acquire the access token on the page. Access token is provided to the users who are owners or admin of the business page.

Facebook allows user to access Graph APIs by providing an access token. User can get access token by three ways:

1. User Access Token
2. App Access Token
3. Page Access Token

Access token is provided to the user after passing the authentication process.

User access token is provided with the data access permission like user data permissions, events, groups, pages, Instagram, videos, and insights. According to your access token provided the user can access the data on Facebook objects.

If anyone wants modify or read app settings, then App access token is required. It is the pre agreement between Facebook and app to read and modify settings on the calls.

To access the data on the business page, Page access token is required. If anyone is the owner or admin of any business page and wants to work on page data like posts data etc. then he has to acquire this type of token. To get the page access token, firstly the person has to acquire the user access token. After getting the user access token person has to get the page access token via Graph API tool.

To extract the data for the present research study, the Investigation has chosen Balvinder's Facebook user account for which user access token is acquired after passing through the authentication by providing userid and password to developers account.

After getting the user access token, next step is to get page access token on the page from where to extract the data. A business page has been created with name Giftdekho with Facebook URL www.facebook. com/giftdekholdh. Being an admin of this business page the investigator has acquired the page access token on this page. Figure 4.5 given below shows the image of getting page access token on the giftdekho page

Figure 4.5: To get the acces token on a Facebook page. (Source:
developers.facebook.com/tools/explorer)

4.2.2.1 Oauth 2.0 Tool

For authentication process Facebook uses Oauth 2.0 tool. This section discusses about this tool.

Oauth 2.0 [137] is an authorization protocol layer, where an end user, the resource owner can grant an access to his protected data stored at the resource server without sharing his username and password with the third party services. This can be achieved by authenticating user credentials directly with the server trusted by authorization server, which issues the access to data by providing the access token.

Oauth 2.0 has four roles:

1. *Resource owner:* It refers to the end user entity who can grant access to protected data/ resources.
2. *Resource Server:* the server which is hosting the end user data/resources and the server will issue the access token to third party to access resources owner data / resources.
3. *Client:* this can be an application or program which sends requests on the behalf of the resource owner for accessing protected data with its authorization.

61

4. *Authorization server:* This is a server that issues access token to the client after authenticating the resource owner.

4.2.3 Extraction of Data using graph API explorer

After passing the authentication process and getting the access token we can extract data using graph API explorer. API is a primary way to get data in and out from the online social networking sites.

Graph API is used to represent the social graph on the Facebook, which represents the information available on the Facebook pages. The social graph is composed of three components

1. **Nodes**: Node represents an individual object on a social graph. For example a user, a business page, an image or any comment.
2. **Edges**: it represents the connections between a collection of objects and a singl object. For example comments on a post, images on a business page.
3. **Fields**: it represents the data about an object. For example page name, description of the business page etc.

4.2.3.1 Usage of node, edge and field

1. **Nodes** can be used to get the data of a specific object on social media. If investigator wants to get data for a post on a page then node will be used.
2. **Edges** can be used to get collections of objects on a single object. If investigator wants to get all the comments data on a post of a business page then, edge will be used.
3. Fields can be used to get Meta data about an object or each object in collection. If investigator wants to get the name of a page then fields will be used.

Facebook Graph API provides http/1.1 for transferring the data and all endpoints require https. To extract the data from Facebook, reading operations begin with node with its unique ID. E.g. A page node with a unique ID can be used to receive the data from Facebook Page.

We can use command:

Get https://graph.facebook.com/<pageID> to retrieve the information about the page.

Nodes in the Facebook have edges, which help in returning the collection of other nodes connected with them. To extract the data using edge, user can use node ID and edge name in the path URL. E.g. to read the post nodes on a page /feed edge is used.

Get http://graph.facebook.com/<pageID>/feed

It retrieves the data in JSON format while extracting the data from Facebook with the nodes and edges you can specify the filters on data. To achieve this fields are used. Fields are node properties. With fields you can specify which field you want to retrieve by using field parameter and listing each field.

e.g. to retrieve about me information one can use : *me/?fields=about*

So with the help of the nodes, edges, and fields user can extract the data from Facebook pages in JSON format.

To retrieve the comments from the post on a page we can use:

Get https://graph.facebook.com/<pageID_postID>/Comments

This command extracts the comments on a particular post given by users as a feedback or review for the post.

4.2.3.2   Extraction of Data from Gift Dekho page

After getting the access token on page, following command was executed in the Facebook Graph API explorer:

1444109289155226_2078984755667673/comments

Where 1444109289155226 is page id and 2078984755667673 is post id for a particular post which makes it a complete node and /comments edge to retrieve the comments from a post.

Figure 4.6: Facebook Page Comments Data Retrieval. (Source: developers.facebook.com/tools/explorer)

4.2.4 Conversion of Data

As shown in the Figure 4.6, Facebook Graph explorer API returns the data in JSON which make it difficult for the end user to read the data in proper format and use it for further processing. So, we need to convert the data into XML. XML is Extensible Markup Language and format provided by XML is easy to use, all the web application development languages accept data in XML format which can be formatted with XSL for better presentation.

To convert the JSON data into XML format python is used. Python is high level object oriented programming language [78]. Python is used for the development of data science program development. Python is free and open source language with large standard library for regular expressions, web browsers, unit testing, email, image manipulation, threading, databases and a lot of other functionality.

Python [124] provides modules and packages which is a collection of python programs used to solve any problem by programming. In this paper we have used xmltodict package to convert JSON code into xml code.

64

Algorithm is given below:

Algorithm: To Convert JSON file to XML format.

Input: This algorithm takes the sample.json file as an input. This file is created from the data extracted from the Facebook page using Graph API Tool Explorer. Data was copied and saved into .json file after providing the root element.

Step 1: import json and import xmltodict

Step 2: with open('sample.json', 'r') as f:

Step3: jsonString = f.read()

Step 4: print('JSON input (input.json):') and print(jsonString)

Step 5: xmlString = xmltodict.unparse(json.loads(jsonString), pretty=True)

Step 6: print('\nXML output(output.xml):') and print(xmlString)

Step7: with open('output.xml', 'w') as f:

Step 8: f.write(xmlString)

Output: this algorithm / program generates the output.xml file, which contain the data in xml file.

Table 4.1 : To Show the .json file and .xml file after conversion.	
Sample.json file	Output.xml file

```
Input.json - Notepad
File Edit Format View Help
{
"message":
{
  "data": [
    {
      "created_time": "2018-12-10T14:30:02+0000",
      "from": {
        "name": "Balvinder Taneja",
        "id": "1444109289155226"
      },
      "message": "learn full course",
      "id": "2078984909000991_2273182602914553"
    },
    {
      "created_time": "2018-02-14T16:48:40+0000",
      "message": "Yes balvinder ji i want to learn",
      "id": "2078984909000991_2079133982319417"
    },
    {
      "created_time": "2018-03-02T07:31:14+0000",
      "message": "Yes",
      "id": "2078984909000991_2086959371536878"
    }
  ],
  "paging": {
    "cursors": {
      "before": "MwZDZD",
      "after": "MQZDZD"
    }
  }
}
}
```

```
C:\python1\output.xml
C:\python1\output.xml
<?xml version="1.0" encoding="UTF-8"?>
<message>
  <data>
    <created_time>2018-12-10T14:30:02+0000</created_time>
    <from>
      <name>Balvinder Taneja</name>
      <id>1444109289155226</id>
    </from>
    <message>learn full course</message>
    <id>2078984909000991_2273182602914553</id>
  </data>
  <data>
    <created_time>2018-02-14T16:48:40+0000</created_time>
    <message>Yes balvinder ji i want to learn</message>
    <id>2078984909000991_2079133982319417</id>
  </data>
  <data>
    <created_time>2018-03-02T07:31:14+0000</created_time>
    <message>Yes</message>
    <id>2078984909000991_2086959371536878</id>
  </data>
  <paging>
    <cursors>
      <before>MwZDZD</before>
      <after>MQZDZD</after>
    </cursors>
  </paging>
</message>
```

4.3 Summary

This chapter has presented the work of extraction of data from the Facebook pages. There are two types of data structured data and unstructured data on the Facebook pages. To extract this data a four step method is explained in this chapter.

It focused on the login authentication of user to get the access token on the page to extract data. It also explained about Oauth2.0 tool of authentication used by the Facebook.

Further it explained the steps used to extract data using Facebook Graph API explorer tool with the help of nodes, edges, and fields. It extracted data from a Facebook page called giftdekho to json file format.

As Facebook provides data in .json format, and XML format is widely accepted on the internet so in the last section it provided with an algorithm to convert the json file into xml format. JSON file and XML file format were shown in a table at the end of this chapter for better understanding.

CHAPTER 5
A PROPOSED MODEL

5.1   Introduction

Data shared by users on the Online Social Networking website is proliferating exponentially. It has generated interest in scientists mind to extract patterns from this data by data mining techniques. As ecommerce companies want to target online social Network users for product promotion, it is desired by these companies to generate useful patterns. Online social Networking websites are collecting data from users in structured and unstructured way. Analyzing these structured data and unstructured data can measure the effectiveness of the campaigns run by e-commerce companies on OSN platforms. Analyzing the unstructured data like comment is tedious, complex and error prone task and it contain lot of noise text.

To achieve the desired results systematic integration of e-commerce and Online Social Network is needed. Therefore, the need for research activities in integration of E-commerce and OSN supporting the unstructured data is apparent.

To accomplish this vision this chapter proposes OSN-ECOM Model that systematically achieve the goal of integration and generate the pattern on unstructured data.

This chapter is divided into three sections. 5.1 is Introduction part. Section 5.2 introduces to OSN-ECOM Model. 5.3 concludes the chapter.

5.2 OSN-ECOMM MODEL

OSN-ECOM Model is proposed with the idea to give an interactive and systematic model that shall move from different phases to uncover the useful patterns. This Proposed Model is exploratory data mining technique that extracts unstructured data from reviews provided in the comment section of OSN websites. The proposed Model proves to be beneficial for the e-commerce companies in the domain Online Social Network page setup, audience building and pattern generation from reviews.

In contrast to the existing model which focuses on case based reasoning for integrating Online Social Networks with e-commerce. The proposed model focuses on initial setup, getting reviews from page audience, extraction of data from page ad pattern generation on five categories from reviews. OSN-E-COM model extracts data using APIs provided by Facebook in XML file and using python language. It tokenizes a string into individual words. After removing noise, stop words, symbols it generates useful patterns by data mining technique.

The Proposed Model comprises of four modules:

- Business Account setup and Audience Building Module.
- Reviews data extraction Module
- Intelligent Review Selection & Pattern Generation Module
- Pattern Analysis and Visualization Module.

Figure 5.1 presents the block diagram of OSN-ECOM Model with its all modules.

First Module BA&ABM, encourages the companies to create setup on Online Social Network and build Followers. Second Module RDEM defines the steps to extract unstructured data provided by page audience in the comment section in the form of reviews.

Third module, IRS&PGM takes input from 2nd module in XML format. It extracts the data from XML file and stores in string format, after filtering and tokenization it generates patterns of data in bad, satisfy, good, excellent and complaint categories. The Fourth module generates percent analysis and visualize the data in BAR Chart using python. Working of each module is described in detail in the upcoming sections.

Phase 1:   Business Account Setup and Audience Building Module.

Phase 2:   Reviews Data Extraction Module.

Phase 3:   Intelligent Review Selection and Pattern Generation Module.

Phase 4:   Pattern Analysis and Visualization

OSN-ECOM Model is represented by the figure 5.1 given below:

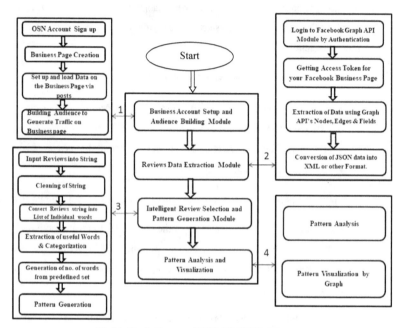

Fig 5.1: Block diagram of OSN-ECOM Model.

5.2.1 Business Account Setup and Audience Building Module (BAS&ABM)

Every e-commerce company on the World Wide Web wants to reach the targeted audience using different channels like search engine, Social Media and e-mail etc. Presence on OSN like Facebook, Twitter, LinkedIn etc. has become essential for promotion. This module covers the four sub-module through which any company can setup business page on OSN like Facebook and build page followers who can like and follow to get notified whenever page updates. Our system achieves this goal through BAS&ABM. A detailed four phased blocked diagram for BAS&ABM is shown in the figure 5.2 below:

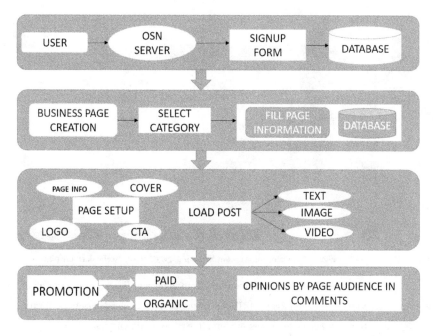

Figure 5.2: Business Account Setup and Audience Building Module

5.2.1.1 OSN Account Sign up

To use the Social Media on World Wide Web, a user needs to create Business account on the Online Social Networking websites like Facebook, Twitter, and LinkedIn etc. First step is to create an account on Facebook by visiting URL www.facebook.com/r.php/. After visiting to the specified webpage the user can register by providing personal information like name, email-id, mobile number, gender, date of birth and secure password for login into the personal account. Figure 5.3 shows the Facebook sign up screen below:

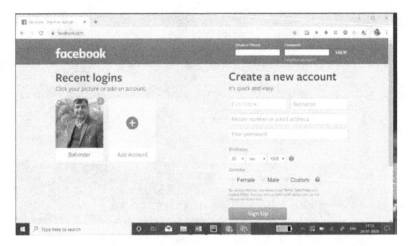

Figure 5.3: Facebook Account Sign up page. (Source: facebook.com/r.php)

To access the created account, the user has to login into Facebook account by providing Facebook userid and password. This personal account is mandatory to perform any type of activity on Facebook. Users are not allowed to create and run a Facebook account at the name of business or company.

Facebook account works on friend of friend model. According to Erdos-Renyi Model people can be friends with anyone at random for newly created account and then account can follow friend of friend model according to small-world effect.

5.2.1.2   Business Page Creation

According to Facebook policy, if any company wants to promote its products or services, they need to create a Facebook Business page. In contrast to personal profile, business page provides boost post option, insights section for analysis, publishing tools for scheduling posts, inbox to interact with page audience and ad center to create beautiful promotional ads. In create->page option, the company can create business page or brand page, community / public figure page.

71

Facebook Business page works on the method of LIKE page. The Online Social Network users who want to follow any page, should like the page to get notifications from the page whenever page updates. Figure 5.4 shows the Business page creation image from Facebook.

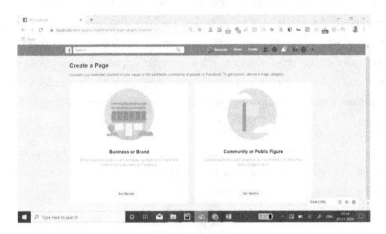

Figure 5.4: Facebook business page creation screen.
(Source: facebook.com/pages/creation/)

From the personal profile Facebook account, admin of the Business page can invite their friends to like the Page. In this way friends on the personal account can help in growing page audience up to 5000, as it is Facebook friend's limit.

5.2.1.3   Setup and load data on Business Page via post

Business page is a tool which represents the company on Online Social Network, so it should be aesthetically designed with essential features. It should act as central hub for any company on OSN for business offers. Business page must be optimized by setting up features provided by Facebook.

Company should update essential information like about you, phone number (s), Email address, location, and working hours. This information helps the page visiting users to know about the company's Meta information

Page visitors can take action by clicking on Call-To-Action button. Facebook provides prominently featured suite of action buttons like book now, contact us, sign up, send message, send email, call now, watch video, learn more, shop now, see offers use app, play game or visit group options to select appropriate options for business page. This button is placed at the top of page and encourage people to contact the company's personnel. Admin must select the page template and action button according to business theme.

A unique and appropriate page name can help the OSN users to locate the page easily on internet. Company can set username for business page by create page@username option on the left of page.

Business page has options to set profile photo and cover photo. Profile photo is generally 170x170 pixel size and company's logo should be set for this. This is an icon that appears every time when any post is created on the page or any interaction with page audience is initiated.

To show your brand in a visual way, at the top of Page Company can set cover photo in a size 820x462 pixels. Cover photo helps branding and depicts about the company's features to draw attention of visiting users.

Facebook also provides the facility to customize business page through template and tabs option in page settings. According to type of business, company can select the template design of business page. Facebook page has various inbuilt templates: shopping, venus, movies, non-profit, politician, services, restaurants & café, video page and standard.

Company can also customize tabs by settings from list of tabs : offers, services, shop, reviews, photos, videos, live videos, events, about, notes, community, groups, info and ads.

Company can also set the roles for team members to handle the page. Page has inbuilt roles like admin, editor, moderator, advertiser, and analyst.

These are the few essential settings for the business page to attract the internet users to like the page. After setting the page next step is to load the information for audience via post.

Facebook allows admin or team members to publish content on the business page via post. Post is a content in the form of photos, video, text, an event or a link. To engage the page visitors, company should create a welcome post and pin it on the top of page, so that it should be always the first post on the business page. Company should post product or service images, meaningful content with call-to-action to generate interest in page visitors to like page and engage them in post.

Page stories also helps to share content, photos and videos for 24 hours' time to bring page audience on journey from start to end of sales funnel.

After posting few posts on the page, company can start building audience for page by inviting Facebook friends, co-workers to like the business page by organic efforts. Company can create ads by boosting any post by paid advertisement. Details of traffic generation is discussed in the next section.

5.2.1.4 Building Audience to Generate Traffic on Business Page

After setting up Facebook business page next step is to build page audience which may regularly visit the page to know about the products or services offered by the company. Users can like the business page and get notified whenever page updates. To build the audience for page there are two ways

1. **Organic** Traffic: it is the number of visitors that visit page without paying or through search result.
2. **Paid Traffic**: it is the number of visitors that visit on a business page by paying to online social networking websites like Facebook. Cost per Click(CPC), Cost per

thousand impressions (CPM) and fixed amount for space on page are the famous paid advertisement techniques available on the internet. Cost per click is the amount that advertiser pays to OSN websites to get click on ad from a user matching the target audience. Cost per mile is the amount paid by the advertiser to OSN website for providing one thousand impressions to the target audience.by offering these paid ads as sponsored ads company can encourage interested users to like their page and become prospectus for future sales.

To run the advertisement on OSN website like Facebook, Instagram etc. company has to run the campaign by selecting on objective and out of the following objective options available:

- Awareness Campaign
- Consideration Campaign
- Conversion Campaign

1. **Awareness Campaign**: This type of campaign can be run by the company, if it wants to generate interest of people in company's product or services. Company can reach maximum number of people by running either brand awareness or reach type campaign under this category.

2. **Consideration Objective:** if a Company wants that people should think about their product or service and they should explore more information about product/service, then this type of campaign objective is suitable. In this category campaign can be run for goals in mind like traffic generation for website, more app installs, to increase post engagements, post likes, offer claims or events responses, to increase video views, for lead generation and get messages from trafiic.

3. **Conversion Objective:** Company can run this type of campaign to encourage the people to buy or use their product or service. Campaign can be run for product catalogue sales or store visits under this category. Conversion campaigns drive valuable actions on your website, app or in messenger.

5.2.1.5   Reactions on Page post

When companies post on the online social networking website like Facebook, the passive type of users just see the post and don't react to the post. But active type of users give reactions in the form to post in the form of pressing like button of different variations of love, haha, wow, sad and anger or as provided by OSN website according to present time. User can share any post in their network or on any page or group. Users can also give reviews or opinion in the comment section provided by OSN website. Opinion provided in the textual format under comment section is active form of click speech. The opinion provided by the users in comment section produces the unstructured data. pattern generation from this unstructured data by data mining techniques to convert into structured form and analysis of this data for decision making and using it for competitive advantage is the objective of current research study.

5.2.2   Reviews Data Extraction Module (RDEM)

RDEM involves the procedure to extract reviews from comment section provided by page audience on Facebook business page in BAS&ABM. It has four sub modules. First sub module covers about the login process into Facebook graph API explorer tool. Second sub module discusses about the Access Token provided by the Facebook to have an access to data on page. Third sub-module pertains to extract unstructured data in comment section of page using API's nodes, edges and fields. This API generates data in json format, which can be copied and saved in .json file. Fourth sub module focuses on converting the .json file into xml file format which is widely used accepted format on the web and supported by all programing languages. A python code is written to convert the .json file into .xml file. Each module is covered in detail in the upcoming sections. A detailed four phased blocked diagram for RDEM is shown in the figure 5.5 below:

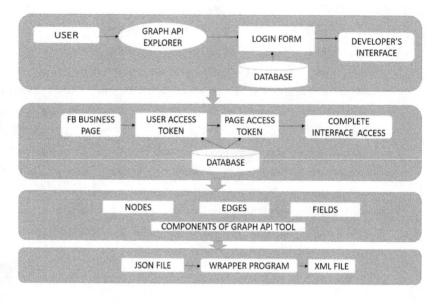

Figure 5.5: Reviews Data Extraction Module (RDEM)

5.2.2.1 Login to Facebook Graph API Module by Authentication

Facebook Graph API explorer is a tool provided for the developers to perform to Graph API queries. Developers can see the query response for any apps according to Facebook developer role. Facebook provides three types of roles 1) ADMIN 2) DEVELOPER 3) TESTER. To use the graph API explorer tool, the user has to login into Facebook developer account as an Admin, Developer or Tester. The account created in BAS&AB module can be used to login into Facebook Graph API tool. This API tool is useful for app development as it inherits all Facebook account app's settings including approved login permissions and other features. Authorised users can run Graph API queries according to app's settings. Graph API tool can be used to generate access token on different pages or apps, build queries, test queries, export query code samples, save queries or generate debug information.

Facebook Graph API explorer tool components:

1) **Application Dropdown**: it displays all the apps on which user have an admin, developer or tester role rights. User can select an app on which he/she wants to work.

2) **Get Token dropdown**: This Dropdown menu allows user to get access on user or app or page. User can uninstall or destroy the current access token.

3) **Login Permission Selector**: it allows the current app user to grant the app specific permissions that is needed. It provides list of every possible permission whenever user requests an access token.

4) **Access Token Field**: in this field information about the current access token with its name is displayed. This access token is included in graph API query.

5) **Query String Field**: it displays the current query. User can run new query or edit the running query through this field.

6) **Node Field Viewer**: in the GET query on a node, this field displays the name of the node and the fields return by the Graph API.

7) **Response window**: it shows the response or request of current query.

8) **Get Code Button**: it generates the sample code based on your current query to give user a starting point.

9) **Copy Debug information button**: it helps user to figure out problem if query is failing and not running successfully.

10) **Save session Button**: it is used to save the state of current query with access token removed.

With the help of Graph API tool and its components query can be executed successfully to extract the data from the business page.

5.2.2.2   Getting Access Token for Facebook Business Page

To have an access to the data on business page through Facebook Graph API explorer tool, users need to have an access token on that page. According to new Facebook policy only admins can have the access to the data on page through this tool. User can get access token in three ways:

1. User Access Token
2. App Access Token
3. Page Access Token

To extract the data from page, company's Business page admin has to get page access token by passing authentication process. Facebook uses Oauth2.0 tool, it is authorization protocol layer where an end user, the resource owner can grant an access to his protected data stored at resource server without sharing his username and password with third party services. This can be achieved by authenticating user credentials directly with server trusted by authorized server, which issues the access to data by providing the access token.

5.2.2.3   Extraction of Data using Graph API's Nodes, Edges & Fields

Facebook Graph API explorer tool has three elements nodes, edges and fields which help to represent or retrieve the data. All the objects are represented as nodes for example page, group, and account. Edge is known as the connection between the two nodes which represent the relationship. For example comments on a particular page's post will be treated as edge. Fields are the data about the node, for example page name or location of the page etc.

With the help of the page name / edge data is extracted in the present research study. The page node giftdekho is used to store and extract the data from page. On a particular page post id is retrieved and then using the pagename / postid and comment edge is used to extract the data from the Facebook page. Extracted data is in JSON format so it needs to be converted into XML format. The conversion process is discussed in next section.

5.2.2.4   Conversion of JSON data into XML or other Format

XML (eXtensible Markupup Langauge) is a format which is used for exchanging the data in standard format. This sub module covers the conversion of json file format into xml file format which is both human readable and machine readable. A python language code was written to convert this.

Facebook Graph API explorer return the data in JSON which make it difficult for end user to read in proper format and use it for further processing. Company needs to convert the data into other format like xml.

To convert the .json file into .xml file format python code/ algorithm   was written. Algorithm is shown in the figure below:

Algorithm: To convert the json file into XML file.

Input: this program takes json files as input which contains the reviews extracted from business page. json and xmltodict python packages are used for this.

Step 1: import two packages : json and xmltodict

Step 2: with open('c:\python1\mi-post-data.json', 'r') as f: jsonString = f.read()

Step 3: print ('JSON input (json file):') , print(jsonString)

Step 4: xmlString = xmltodict.unparse(json.loads(jsonString), pretty=True)

Step 5: print('\nXML output(output.xml):'), print(xmlString)

Step 6: with open('c:\python1\mi-post-output.xml', 'w') as f: f.write(xmlString)

Output: The xml file containing the data in the XML format is generated by this algorithm.

5.2.3 Intelligent Review Selection and Pattern Generation Module (IRS & PGM)

IRS & PG module receives the data from RDEM in xml format, convert xml data into string and it generates pattern from data after passing through various processes. This module is divided into six sub modules.

First sub module receives the data from previous and stores the data into string format using python language. Second sub module describes the steps to remove special symbols from the string like (? . ,) etc. Third sub module focuses on the technique of tokenization words for ontology matching. Fourth sub module focuses on the elimination of stop words from the list of individual words. This module also describes the five categories on which various patterns will be generated. Fifth sub module explains the python program to calculate the number of words which match with the category words. Sixth sub module focuses on uncovering the hidden patterns in the reviews provided by the page audience by using the data received from fifth sub module. Each sub module will be discussed in details in the coming sections. A detailed four phased blocked diagram for IRS&PGM is shown in the figure 5.6 below:

81

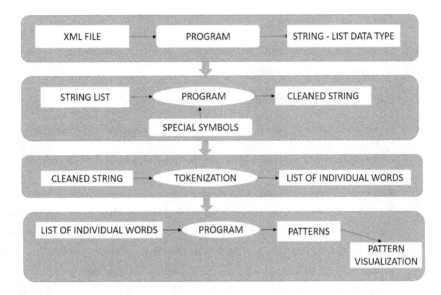

Figure 5.6: Intelligent Review Selection and Pattern Generation Module (IRS & PGM)

5.2.3.1 Input Reviews into String

Data provided by RDE Module is in xml format, which stores the data in tags. To generate useful patterns data inside the tags must be extracted into string to perform the operations. To convert the xml data into string a python code was executed. An algorithm for the same given below:

Algorithm: To Read the XML file and stores reviews into string list.

Input: This program takes the xml file generated in the previous section as an input.

Step 1: comment = []

Step 2: tree = etree.parse("output.xml')

Step 3: root = tree.getroot()

Step 4: for child in root: for subelem in child: if (subelem.tag == 'message'): comment.append(subelem.text)

Step 5: comment = map(lambda x: x.lower(), comment)

Step 6: comment1 = [], for x in comment: comment1.append(x), print (comment1)

Output: This program is used to generate the string list by reading all the comments from the xml file.

An XML file containing the reviews and other data is given as input to this sub module. It uses the xml.etree.ElementTree API to process the XML data and stores the reviews in two dimensional python list in string format. This Program uses the ElementTree parse() function to generate a tree structure for XML program. Starting from the root of the tree program creates a two-dimensional list and append each and every review from xml file into string. List. As reviews given in xml file are in English language, the string list is further converted into lower case which makes the comparison easy. A lower() function of python language is used to convert all the data into lowercase string data.

Now string list containing the comments is ready and ready to pass to next sub module.

5.2.3.2   Cleaning of String

Data stored in the previous module in a python list contain strings in English language, which may contain special characters, punctuation marks, symbols etc. these symbols are not useful for pattern generation as only useful words are required.

This sub module removes the special character or symbols from the string list. A python program / algorithm is written and executed to remove special character/symbols and a list of useful words can be generated by executing the program. An algorithm for the same given below:

Algorithm: To remove special characters / symbols from string.

Input: This algorithm takes the string list as input to the program.

Step1: i = 0;

Step 2: while i < len(comment1):   print(comment1[i])

 Step 3: for char in '?.!,/:;':   comment1[i] = comment1[i].replace(char,' ')

   print(comment1[i]) ,   i = i + 1 Step 4: end;

Output: The String List is regenerated after the cleaning of special symbols and characters by replacing it with white spaces.

This python code read the data from list and find special characters in the string. If there exists any special character it use the list replace function to replace special character with single space. After removing the special symbols from string list now list is cleaned and ready to pass to the next phase of tokenization.

5.2.3.3 Convert Reviews String into List of Individual Words

After cleaning the string list, as required by the present research study a process of tokenization is needed. Tokenization process is splitting the sentence or string into individual words. For example a string "product is very good" after tokenization becomes "product", "is", "very", "good" words list.

A python code was written to read the strings from list and split into individual words. A two dimensional list is created to store the individual words. Out of two dimensions, one dimension is used to store the words from single comment and second is used for all the comments.

split() function is used to split the string or sentence from review into individual words. append() function is used to insert the individual word into newly created list. An algorithm for the same given below:

84

Algorithm for creating of two dimensional list from comments of words know as tokenization.

Input: This algorithm takes the cleaned string list as an input for the tokenization.

Step 1: commentlist=[] is declared for creating two dimensional list, which stores the individual words after tokenization.

Step 2: Commentlist1 list of string is received from previous sub module.

Step 3: While j < len(comment1): loop is run to visit each and every review comment in the commentlist1.

Step 4: commentlist[j] = comment1[j].split() code is used to split j^{th} comment in commentlist1into individual words and store into commentlist[j] j^{th} location. Starting value of j is 0. Value of j moves from 0 to length of commentlist1.

Step 5: commentlist.append([]), is used to append the sub list on each loop counter.

Output: a two-dimensional list is generated from the string list after tokenisation to store the individual words.

After the full loop and code is executed, a two dimensional list containing individual words is generated which contains the useful words.

5.2.3.4 Extraction of Useful Words & Categorization

The words stored in the python two-dimensional list contain all the words generated from the comment section. Some words may be unuseful in this unstructured data, which may generate noise in text. To eliminate the noise from text words, stop words list was created. By using the python code, these stop words were removed from the list and a two dimensional list with useful words was generated.

85

Stop words are the useless words and does not carry any weightage in the pattern generation. List of stop words are shown in the Figure 5.7 given below:

Stop words:

[',','a','about','above','after','again','against','all','am','an','and','any','are','
as','at','be','because','been','before','being','below','between','both','but','
by','can','did','do','does','doing','done','down','during','each','few','for','fro
m','further','had','has','have','having','he','her','here','hers','herself','him','
himself','his','how','i','if','in','into','is','it','it','its','itself','just','me','more','m
ost','my','myself','no','nor','now','of','off','on','once','only','or','other','our',
'ours','ourselves','out','over','own','same','she','should','so','some','such','
than','that','the','their','theirs','them','themselves','then','there','these','th
ey','this','those','through','to','too','under','until','up','very','was','we','wer
e','what','when','where','which','while','who','whom','why','will','with','yo
u','yours','yours','yourself','yourselves' ']

Figure 5.7: List of stop words

Removing of Stop words: As we know, stop words are not useful in decision making or pattern generation. To remove the stop words a list of stop words is created as shown in Figure 24 above.

A python code is written to generate a two-dimensional list after filtering the stop words. An algorithm for the same given below:

Removal of Stop Words

Algorithm: To Remove Stop Words from List.

Input: This algorithm takes the commentlist [] list as input which stores the words extracted from the reviews provided by page audience. It also takes the stopwords list , which contains the unuseful words.

Step 1: Filtercomment=[], a filtercomment list was created to store the words after removal of stop words.

Step 2: K=0, is a counter to run loop.

Step 3: While (): to run the loop to visit each and every word in the comment list. Comment list is the list of words received from the previous sub module.

Step 4: For any word in commentlist at the kth position, k starting from 0. Word is compared with stop word, if it is not a stop word then word is appended in the filter commentlist otherwise move to next word for comparison and so....on.

Step 5: After visiting all the words in commentlist a list with useful words is created by appending the useful words in filtercomment list.

Output: From the above algorithm a list filtercomment is generated which stores all the useful words after removing the stop words from the inputted list.

These useful words are generated after removing the stop words were used to generate patterns using data mining.

User can give reviews in English language. Matching technique is used to compare each word with vocabulary of a domain. A set of words for each category is clustered. A Python code was written which generated the total number of bad, satisfied, good, excellent, and complaint category words. A list in Python was used to store these numbers. Classification and clustering of words was obtained by referring to the English dictionary and words net list.

The present research study has classified five categories in which any word from comment can fall. These categories are Bad, Satisfy, Good, Excellent and Complaint.

➢ **Bad Category Words**: When any user shares his/her review in comment section and provides bad words in the reviews. Different users use different vocabulary synonyms to express their views. A list of bad words synonyms is created so that bad category pattern is easily generated. A list is given below in the Figure 5.8 below:

• Bad words =

['adverse','amateurish','apologetic','awful','bad','bent','bogus','careless', 'coarse','criminal','crooked','crude','decayed','decomposed','defective','de ficient','dirty','disagreeable','dud','evil','fake','false','faulty','filthy','fraudule nt','frightful','gammy','grim','guilt-ridden', 'guilty', 'harmful', 'hurtful', 'immortal','imperfect','inappropriate','indecent','inferior','invalid','knacker ed','mouldy','nasty','negligent','not upto par', 'not upto scratch', 'off', 'offensive', 'penitent', 'poor', 'profane', 'putrefied', 'regretful', 'regrettable' ,'remorseful', 'repentant' , 'rotten', 'rude', 'shamefaced', 'sinful', 'smutty', 'sorry', 'spurious', 'substandard', 'terrible', 'unfavourable', 'unfortunate', 'unhealthy', 'unlucky', 'unpleasant', 'unpropitious', 'unsatisfactory', 'unsuitable', 'untoward', 'unwelcome', 'vulgar', 'wicked', 'worthless']

Figure 5.8: list of Bad Words Category.

➤ **Good Category Words**: When any user share his/her review in comment section and provides Good words in the reviews. Different users use different vocabulary synonyms to express their views. A list of Good words synonyms is created so that Good category pattern is easily generated. A list is given below in the Figure 5.9 below:

•Good words =

['able', 'acceptable', 'accomplished', 'appetizing', 'authentic', 'best', 'bonafide', 'brill', 'brilliant', 'capable', 'cheerful', 'clean', 'competent', 'convincing', 'cracking', 'delicious', 'enjoyable', 'ethical', 'expert', 'fine', 'fit', 'generous', 'genuine', 'gifted' 'good', 'great', 'healthy', 'important', 'jolly', 'kind', 'kind-hearted', 'knowledgeable', 'legitimate', 'lovely', 'lusty', 'mouth watering', 'nice', 'ok', 'outstanding', 'palatable', 'pleasant', 'powerful', 'proficient' ,'quality' ,'rich', 'right', 'righteous', 'robust', 'skilled', 'smart, 'smashing', 'sound', 'sterling' ,'strong', 'super', 'sweet', 'talented', 'tasty' ,'tip top', 'toothsome', 'upright', 'valid', 'virtuous', 'wonderful', 'worthy']

Figure 5.9: List of good Category Words

➤ **Satisfactory Category Words**: When any user shares his/her review in comment section and provides satisfactory words in the reviews. Different users use different vocabulary synonyms to express their views. A list of satisfactory words synonyms is created so that satisfactory category pattern is easily generated. A list is given below in the Figure 5.10 below:

Satisfactory words =

['adequate', 'average', 'competent', 'convenient', 'decent', 'fair', 'moderate', 'reasonable', 'satisfy', 'sufficient', 'suitable']

Figure 5.10: List of Satisfactory words

➢ **Excellent Category Words**: When any user shares his/her review in comment section and provides excellent words in the reviews. Different users use different vocabulary synonyms to express their views. A list of excellent words synonyms is created so that excellent category pattern is easily generated. A list is given below in the Figure 5.11 below:

• Excellent words =

['admirable', 'splendid', 'ace', 'awesome', 'champion', 'excellent', 'exceptional', 'fab', 'fantastic', 'first rate', 'magnificent', 'magic', 'marvellous', 'matchless', 'mind blowing', 'outstanding', 'perfect', 'sublime', 'superb', 'superior', 'superlative', 'swell', 'terrific', 'tremendous', 'wonderful', 'super']

Figure 5.11: List of Excellent Category Words

➢ **Complaint Category Words**: When any user shares his/her review in comment section and provides complaint words in the reviews. Different users use different vocabulary synonyms to express their views. A list of Complaint words synonyms is created so that Complaint category pattern is easily generated. A list is given below in the Figure 5.12 below:

- **Complaint words** =

['accusation','beef','bug','cavil','charge','complaint','criticism','disapprov al','dissatisfaction','fulmination','fuss','grievance','gripe','grouch','grous e','grumble','lurgy','moan','muttering','objection','outcry','problem','pro test','protestation','quibble','remonstrance','trouble','upset','whine','wh inge','wog','yike']

Figure 5.12: List of Complaint Category Words.

This sub module covered the generation of useful words after removing the stop words and classification of words in five categories were generated. In the next sub module category wise pattern words will be generated.

5.2.3.5 Generation of no. of Words from Predefined Set

The list of useful words generated from the previous sub module contains the words which fall in the bad, good, satisfactory, excellent or complaint category. This module focuses on generating the number of words in each category from the list.

For example, it will calculate the number of bad category words from useful words list, good category words, excellent category words or complaint category words.

To generate the number of words algorithm is written and five lists were generated from the program for each category. 5 Algorithms for each category is listed and explained below:

1. Generation of Bad Category Words

Algorithm: To Generate the Bad category words

Input: This algorithm takes the filtercomment [] list as input which stores the useful words from the reviews provided by page audience. it also takes the badwords list , which contains the synonyms words.

Step 1: badwordcounter = 0, a variable to store the number of bad words.

Step 2: badwordfiltercomment = [], list to store the bad category words.

Step 3: while k < len (filtercomment): Loop to visit each and every word in the filtercomment list.

Step4: For w in filtercomment[k]: if w in badwords: badwordfiltercomment[k].append(w) , this code will visit the kth element in the list and compare word with bad words category, if it matches the word in bad word category set then word will be appended in the badwordfiltercomment list at kth position and badwordcouter is incremented by 1.

Step 5: Otherwise loop counter incremented by 1 with k = k + 1.

Output: From the above algorithm a list badwordfiltercomment stores all the bad category words. badwordcounter stores the number of words in the badwordfiltercomment list.

---

2. Generation of Good Category words

Algorithm: To Generate the Good category words.

Input: This algorithm takes the filtercomment [] list as input which stores the useful words from the reviews provided by page audience. It also takes the goodwords list , which contains the synonyms words.

Step 1: goodwordcounter = 0, a variable to store the number of good words.

Step 2: goodwordfiltercomment = [], list to store the good category words.

Step 3: while k < len (filtercomment): Loop to visit each and every word in the filtercomment list.

Step4: For w in filtercomment[k]: if w in goodwords: goodwordfiltercomment[k].append(w) , this code will visit the kth element in the list and compare word with good words category, if it matches the word in good word category set then word will be appended in the goodwordfiltercomment list at k^{th} position and goodwordcouter is incremented by 1.

Step 5: Otherwise loop counter incremented by 1 with k = k + 1.

Output: From the above algorithm a list goodwordfiltercomment stores all the good category words. goodwordcounter stores the number of words in the goodwordfiltercomment list.

---

3. Generation of Satisfactory Category words

Algorithm: To Generate the Satisfactory Category Words.

Input: This algorithm takes the filtercomment [] list as input which stores the useful words from the reviews provided by page audience. It also takes the satisfactorywords list, which contains the synonyms words.

Step 1: sswordcounter = 0, a variable to store the number of satisfactorywords words.

Step 2: sswordfiltercomment = [], list to store the satisfactorywords category words.

Step 3: while k < len (filtercomment): Loop to visit each and every word in the filtercomment list.

Step4: For w in filtercomment[k]: if w in satisfactorywords: sswordfiltercomment[k].append(w) , this code will visit the kth element in the list and compare word with satisfactory words category, if it matches the word in satisfactory word category set then word will be appended in the sswordfiltercomment list at k^{th} position and sswordcouter is incremented by 1.

Step 5: Otherwise loop counter incremented by 1 with k = k + 1.

Output: From the above algorithm a list sswordfiltercomment stores all the satisfactorywords category words. sswordcounter stores the number of words in the sswordfiltercomment list.

4. Generation of excellent Category words

Algorithm: To generate the excellent category words

Input: This algorithm takes the filtercomment [] list as input which stores the useful words from the reviews provided by page audience. it also takes the excellent list , which contains the synonyms words.

Step 1: exwordcounter = 0, a variable to store the number of excellent words.

Step 2: exwordfiltercomment = [], list to store the excellent category words.

Step 3: while k < len (filtercomment): Loop to visit each and every word in the filtercomment list.

Step4: For w in filtercomment[k]: if w in excellentwords: exwordfiltercomment[k].append(w) , this code will visit the kth element in the list and compare word with excellent words category, if it matches the word in excellent word category set then word will be appended in the exwordfiltercomment list at k^{th} position and exwordcouter is incremented by 1.

Step 5: Otherwise loop counter incremented by 1 with k = k + 1.

Output: From the above algorithm a list exwordfiltercomment stores all the excellent category words. exwordcounter stores the number of words in the exwordfiltercomment list.

93

5. Generation of Complaint Category words

Algorithm: To Generate the Complaint Category words

Input: This algorithm takes the filtercomment [] list as input which stores the useful words from the reviews provided by page audience. It also takes the complaintwords list, which contains the synonyms words.

Step 1: cwwordcounter = 0, a variable to store the number of Complaint words.

Step 2: badwordfiltercomment = [], list to store the Complaint category words.

Step 3: while k < len (filtercomment): Loop to visit each and every word in the filtercomment list.

Step4: For w in filtercomment[k]: if w in complaintwords: cwwordfiltercomment[k].append(w) , this code will visit the kth element in the list and compare word with complaint words category, if it matches the word in complaint word category set then word will be appended in the cwwordfiltercomment list at k^{th} position and cwwordcouter is incremented by 1.

Step 5: Otherwise loop counter incremented by 1 with k = k + 1.

Output: From the above algorithm a list cwwordfiltercomment stores all the complaint category words. cwwordcounter stores the number of words in the cwwordfiltercomment list.

5.2.3.6 Pattern Generation

Motive of the present research study is to uncover the patterns using data mining technique. Using the exploratory data mining technique patterns are generated from the reviews provided by the users. Using the above sub modules total number of words from each category were generated and individual list was also generated which stored the actual words used by the reviewer.

Further this module focused to uncover the hidden patterns after calculating the number of words from each category. Numbers from each category were converted into percentages.

To generate the patterns total number of words is to be counted with the following formula:

total=badwordcounter+sswordcounter+goodwordcounter+exwordcounter+cwwordcounter

after calculating the total number of words, percentage of each category words is counted by applying the following formaula:

pbad=(badwordcounter/total)*100

pss=(sswordcounter/total)*100

pgood=(goodwordcounter/total)*100

pex=(exwordcounter/total)*100

pcw=(cwwordcounter/total)*100

Where pbad, pss, pgood, pex, pcw are the variables to store the percentage in bad category, satisfactory category, good category, excellent category and complaint category respectively.

These badwordcounter, sswordcounter, goodwordcounter, exwordcounter, cwwordcounter, pbad, pss, pgood, pex and pcw store the pattern data which was hidden in the reviews provided by the page visitors. These patterns are generated from the present research study by the data mining techniques.

5.2.4   Pattern Analysis and Visualization Module

After getting the pattern data from the previous module, this module's work is to analyze the hidden pattern generated from the reviews for the benefits of the organization. This module has two sub modules. First sub module focuses on the percentage analysis on the pattern generated and second sub module focuses on the visualization of pattern using Graphical method.

5.2.4.1   Pattern Analysis

This sub module discussed about the percentage analysis method to analyse the patterns generated. Percentage analysis method is used to express the relative frequency of data on the data points. These percentage frequency distribution are displayed as bar charts or in the form of tables.

The process used for creating frequency distribution involves identifying the no. of total observations, then counting the total no. of observations within each data point. Finally percentage distribution are calculated by dividing the no. of observations within each data point to total no. of observations.

In the present research work, pbad, pss, pgood, pex, pcw are the five variables which store the percentage distribution for the bad, satisfactory, good, and excellent and complaint categories.

Companies are interested in the insights provided by any wrapper program. Pattern analysis is the process by which companies can observe and analyse the different patterns generated using data mining techniques. In the present study unstructured data is converted into structured data on the five categories of bad, good, satisfactory, excellent and complaint category. Basically when reviews are provided by the page audience on product/ service Post Company may be interested in knowing the data about the reviews. Company may want to see that how many people have given good reviews, how many have given bad reviews, how many have given excellent reviews, how many have given satisfactory reviews and how many have given the complaining reviews. Because these

96

reviews provided by the page audience are viewed by the public on the internet and in today's era it definitely influences the buying decision of another user on the internet.

As e-commerce companies are targeting the online users for their product promotion, reviews provided by people in the comment section surely influence the sale of any product. With the current research study wrapper program they can generate the patterns from the reviews, analyse them and use to improve if negative reviews are provided by the people or target the more internet users if positive feedback is provided by the users.

Analysis of pattern gives idea to the company about how many people are liking and how many are disliking the product. Instead of analysing the data on numbers in any data set, percentage analysis statistical method gives clear information on 100 point scale. To generate the percentage frequency distribution an algorithm is written and program is run in the python programming language.

5.2.4.2   Pattern Visualization by Graph

This sub module focussed on the steps to generate and analyse the bar chart from patterns of data uncovered. It also discussed how visualization is helpful for decision making. As discussed in the previous section about the percentage frequency distribution analysis and number frequency distribution analysis. The bar charts are generated in both the patterns.

For the different categories different colour scheme is used. For the Bad category red color graph is used, for the satisfactory color of graph is yellow, for good and excellent category green color is used and for complaining category red color is used. Whenever a graph is generated from the pattern data in number and in percentage if more green bars are there, it means the reviews provided by the users are in good or excellent category and people are liking the product or services. If more bars are in red color that means people are not liking the product, which can lead to loss in business sale. If yellow color bar is high that means people are satisfactory about the product or service but not enthusiastic.

Pattern Visualisation is providing a clear picture about the product reviews on the OSN network and these insights can be useful for the business economic value. At a glance this can help users and companies to analyse the data about the product.

To show the patterns in graphical form, bar graphs and percentage bar graphs on the two posts from the Facebook page has been generated. This has been exemplified in the figures 5.13, 5.14, 5.15 and 5.16 below:

Graphical Representation on no. of comments in each Category

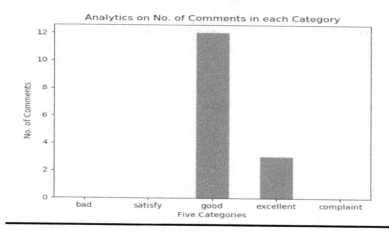

Figure 5.13: Pattern Visualization on number of reviews in each Category from Facebook page post number 697232147326696_7501270587038.

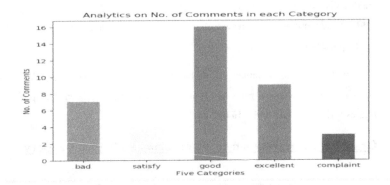

Figure 5.14: Pattern Visualization on number of reviews in each Category from Facebook page post number 697232147326696_1036505913399316.

Graphical Presentation on Percentage Analysis

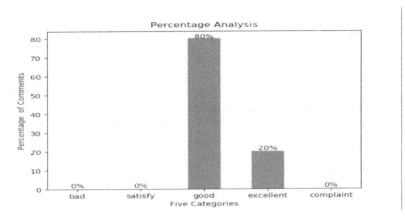

Figure 5.15: Pattern Visualization on percentage calculated on number of reviews in each Category from Facebook page post number 697232147326696_7501270587038

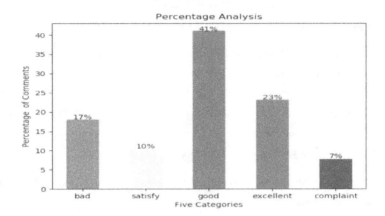

Figure 5.16: Pattern Visualization on percentage calculated on number of reviews in each Category from Facebook page post number 697232147326696_1036505913399316.

5.3 Conclusion

This chapter has presented the proposed model of the research work. The proposed model has 4 modules:

1. Business Account Setup and Audience Building Module.
2. Reviews Data Extraction Module.
3. Intelligent Review Selection and Pattern Generation Module.
4. Pattern Analysis and Visualization

Business Account Setup and Audience Building Module covered the Account setup on the social media and Audience building on social media. It covered the detail about how to setup a personal account, business page, loading data on the business page by creating posts, building strong audience for promoting it to generate traffic and reactions on the posts in the form of likes, shares and comments.

Reviews Data Extraction_Module presented steps to extract the data from the business pages by using the Graph API Tool. Graph API Tool provides the primary data with the

100

help of nodes and the edges in the form of json file format. This module also presented an algorithm to convert the json file data in standard xml file format.

Intelligent Review Selection and Pattern Generation Module presented the 9 algorithms which covered reading xml data and storing into Python list, cleaning of symbols from the string list, converting string into lust of individual words by the tokenization techniques, removal of stop words from the list, generation of Bad category words, generation of Good category words, generation of Satisfactory words, generation of Excellent category words, generation of Complaint category words.

The purpose of this module is to generate the patterns from the unstructured data received in the xml format.

Pattern Analysis and Visualization Module: Pattern generated can only be useful if it is analyzed properly for decision making. This module presented the data in visual format like bar charts and presented the percentage analysis technique for better understanding.

All four Modules presented the Proposed Model in this chapter effectively.

CHAPTER 6
EXISTING MODEL vs. PROPOSED MODEL

6.1 Introduction

The Proposed OSN-ECOM Model has been designed and implemented using the python language. It has also used the concepts of JSON and XML. The modules have been implemented with Facebook Graph API Explorer and Facebook business page. The present research work has used Pycharm editor and windows 10 with i3 Intel processor.

This chapter focused on the comparison of proposed model with the existing model in the integration of Online Social Network and E-commerce. The existing model is based on the case based reasoning (CBR Model) whereas the proposed model works on the reviews provided by the page audience on the online social Networking websites.

This chapter is divided into 4 sections. Section 6.1 describes the introduction. Section 6.2 presents the CBR model of integration of OSN and e-commerce. Section 6.3 presents the comparison between CBR model and proposed model of present research work. Section 6.4 presents the conclusion of this chapter.

6.2 What CBR model Says?

According to integrating online social networking with e-commerce based on CBR two persons with similar interests have similar online purchasing behaviors.

Sun [127] defined the architecture of integrating OSN with e-commerce based on the case based reasoning. Using the assumption that if F1 and F2 are two friends on the Facebook website and F1 is similar to F2, then F1 and F2 have the similar purchasing behavior on e-commerce websites. So CBR says similar online social network friends have similar online purchasing behavior.

6.3 Comparison between Proposed model and CBR Model

➢ In CBR model two online social friends are required where one friend is similar to other, whereas in proposed model single user can read the reviews provided by other known or unknown users.

➢ CBR model is experience based reasoning model between two friends to reach to any purchasing behavior, whereas proposed model is review based purchasing influence between known or unknown online users.

➢ CBR model is similarity based reasoning on the online e-commerce purchasing behavior between two friends, whereas proposed model is also similarity based model for purchasing the same or similar product or service between known or unknown people, but reviews may have influence on the purchasing decision.

➢ CBR Model has two stages

1. Case retrieval, and
2. Case Adaption

Whereas according to proposed model the user has to go through four stages of implementation to get the product / service review.

1. Business Account Setup and Audience Building Module.
2. Review Data Extraction Module.
3. Intelligence Review Selection and Pattern Generation Module.
4. Pattern Analysis and Visualization.

This Proposed model also provides insights to companies after passing through four stages.

The proposed model provides pattern visualization, where unstructured comment data is represented in structured bar graph to provide clear understanding of bad, satisfactory, good, and excellent and complaint categories. Hence, it is analyzed that proposed model is better than the existing model.

6.4 Conclusion

This chapter has presented the comparison between Case Base Reasoning (CBR) model of Integration with the proposed model of present research work. CBR model has two stages whereas proposed model has four phases to achieve the required goal. CBR model only gives results for two similar friends with similar behavior whereas proposed model gives results on the basis of reviews provided by the online social network users in the comment section. The reviews provided by the users may influence the purchasing decision of other users. With pattern visualization it is analyzed that the proposed model is better than the existing CBR model.

CHAPTER 7
CONCLUSION AND FUTURE SCOPE

The theme of this thesis is generation of social commerce. The actual action taken by integrating the online social network and e-commerce. Unstructured data is generated from the social media Facebook business page and by using the wrapper program, it was converted into structured data on five categories. The work undertaken in this thesis not only generated the structured data patterns but also analysis of pattern and visualization of patterns is discussed. At the end a whole model for integration of OSN & e-commerce is developed.

A summary of proposed model for the OSN & e-commerce, the main findings with respect to the identified research objectives and questions, research contributions and possible future scope are therefore presented in this chapter.

This chapter is divided into four sections. Section 7.1 gives the summary of proposed model for OSN and E-commerce. Section 7.2 presents the main findings of the research work. Section 7.3 reemphasized the research contribution. Finally some directions for future research are discussed in the section 7.4.

7.1 Summary

The objective of proposed OSN-E-COMM model is to benefit the companies and users to observe, analyze and to take action according to reviews provided by the OSN business page audience on a product or service post.

OSN-E-COMM proposed model comprises of four main parts: 1) Business Account Setup and Audience Building Module. 2) Reviews Data Extraction Module. 3) Intelligent Review Selection and Pattern Generation Module. 4) Pattern Analysis and Visualization

Business Account Setup and Audience Building Module have four sub modules 1) OSN Account Sign up: 2) Business Page Creation 3) Setup and load data on Business Page via post 4) Building Audience to Generate Traffic on Business Page.

This module is basically a setup module. All the account login setup, business page setup, creating posts and building page audience are covered in this module. This module also generates the reviews from the end users on a business post in the form of unstructured textual data.

Reviews Data Extraction Module have four sub modules 1) Login to Facebook Graph API Module by Authentication 2) Getting Access Token for your Facebook Business Page 3) Extraction of Data using Graph API's Nodes, Edges & Fields 4) Conversion of JSON data into XML format.

This module uses the data generated from the first module in the comment section. By passing through an authentication process and using Facebook Graph API explorer tool it extracts the data into .json format. This json file is finally converted into XML file, a standard format widely accepted on the internet.

Intelligent Review Selection and Pattern Generation Module have six sub modules 1) Input Reviews into String: 2) Cleaning of String 3) Convert Reviews String into List of Individual words 4) Extraction of Useful Words & Categorization 5) Generation of no. of Words from Predefined Set 6) Pattern Generation

This module focuses on the pattern generation from the data extracted in XML format. Data generated in XML format is converted into string data type. The string is then split into a list of individual words and stored into List data type. To extract the useful words only, list is filtered by eliminating the stop words. After eliminating the stop words, string list of useful words is put into comparing process to generate bad, satisfying, good excellent, complaining or none category words. All the words in the list are compared with a predefined set of synonym words. From all the review comments, an overall pattern is generated to tell that how many users have given bad, satisfying, good or excellent category comments. It also generates the complaining comments, so that the company can see how many users are complaining online on social media.

Pattern Analysis and Visualization have two sub modules 1) Pattern Analysis 2) Pattern Visualization by Graph.This module focuses on the Pattern analysis. Data is generated in different categories and percent analysis method is used to analyze the patterns. To view the data in visualization form bar charts are generated in frequency and percentage. As these patterns have uncovered the hidden patterns by data mining, these patterns can help the companies in product improvement or any type of decision making.

7.2 Main Findings of Study

As stated in the chapter 1, the key aim of the work discussed in the thesis is to represent relationship between Online Social Network and E-commerce using Data Mining with the objectives 1) To study and evaluate the existing models relating to e-Commerce and Online Social Network. 2) To extract different patterns of data from e-Commerce and Online Social Network pages. 3) To propose a model to represent relationship between e-Commerce and Online Social Network. 4) To compare the proposed model with existing models. In this section main findings of the experimentation are discussed in the context of the research issues central to this thesis:

1. **Data Extraction and Conversion:** The procedure and algorithm used in the RDE is useful to extract the data from a post on the Facebook page. The procedure used is helpful in extracting all the comments from a post in one go. The Graph API is used for this purpose. The algorithm used in the module can be used convert the data in JSON format to XML format. These findings can help the companies to convert the data from JSON to XML widely accepted format.

2. **Categorization:** Patterns are generated on five categories by IRS & PG module. Five categories are made by grouping the synonyms in bad, satisfactory, good, and excellent and complaint words. Category wise analysis gives clear idea about the patterns for making strategies for future promotions and decision making.

3. **Pattern Generation:** The identification of patterns using the IRS & PG module allows companies and end users to discover hidden information in social network data. With tokenization, categorization and wrapper algorithm the conversion process

107

for the unstructured data into structured data can take place smoothly. To extract the large no. of reviews provided by the page audience, Graph API is used with its nodes, edges, and field elements. It generates the patterns on the Bad, Satisfactory, Good, Excellent and Complaint categories for analyzing the result according to company's interest.

4. **Interpretation of Patterns:** The Grouping and Categorization of words under the IRS & PG module provides a mechanism to analyze the reviews by grouping synonyms words under different categories. The grouping of words under one category allows companies and users to identify the patterns that exist in a set of data point. With the color code given to bar charts generated from data, pattern interpretation can be understood easily.

5. **Visualization:** The proposed PA & V module was used to display the Bar charts on the number of words and sets. The benefit of visualization is that it gives better interpretation of the pattern generated. In the case of PA & V module the information is represented in the form of Bar Charts with different color code. For the Bad category red color graph was used, for the satisfactory color of graph is yellow, for good and excellent category green color was used and for complaining category red color was used.

Thus, given the above findings, the proposed mechanisms incorporated into the OSN-ECOM model can address the issues by integrating the OSN and ecommerce on reviews. It is also helpful in finding the answers that come in the users mind before purchasing a product or service online. Reviews analysis in structured way can help the online users about the product quality and features. With respect to the research issues, the proposed model ensures the quality and effectiveness for integration of online social network & ecommerce and reviews pattern generation on some of the following features:

1. **Scalability:** The proposed model is able to process large and small data sets of reviews available on the OSN page.

2. **Flexibility:** This proposed model can be applied to different social media platforms to generate patterns. This model is flexible enough to generate patterns.

3. **Accuracy:** once data is available in XML format, the proposed model can re-use to generate patterns from any post of any page by the concept of re-usability.

4. **Reusability:** Analysis of the generated patterns produced by the proposed model with the support of Intelligence Review system indicated that correct patterns were generated and visualized.

5. **Presentation:** The pattern generated by the proposed model presents the patterns in color coding scheme for the better understanding in a glance view.

7.3 Research Contribution

The main contribution of the present research work can be summarized as follows:

1. A mechanism for data extraction from OSN pages in the specified format.

2. A mechanism for efficiently converting data from one data format to standard acceptable data type to generate the patterns from Online Social Networks.

3. A mechanism for grouping the words under the different and appropriate categories for better insights and analysis.

4. A pattern generation mechanism to convert unstructured data of reviews to structured data on the different five predefined categories.

5. Visualization of patterns on the Bar Chart with color coding to analyze the patterns.

6. A four phased complete model representation from phase 1 to Phase 4 with its implementation procedures.

7.4 Research Future Direction

A strong integration model for pattern generation from review has been established. The procedures with algorithm are incorporated in the proposed model for quality work. The research work undertaken has raised a number of promising future directions to enhance the OSN-ECOM model as follows:

1. **Sentiment Analysis of Unstructured Data**: the proposed model presented the patterns from opinion provided by the OSN users in an effective way. The

sentiment of the users are not attached in the present research study. The future researchers can add the sentiment analysis on unstructured data.

2. **Sentiment Orientation on Reviews:** in the present research study, the reviews provided by the users are considered as a true & original opinion. Currently there is no mechanism to check the authenticity of the reviews provided by the users. There are number of third parties which are providing fake reviews on the post, which can mislead or make wrong impression in the user's mind. The future researchers can work in this direction to provide a correct and authentic review.

3. **Sentiment Lexicon Expansion**: As present research work categorizes the words on five categories based on opinion synonyms available in the dictionary. The present research study categories can be expanded with sentiment lexicons, which can expand the synonyms words on sentiment basis.

4. **Internet Language**: The language words used for providing an opinion in the form of reviews are becoming a challenging issue. People are writing in short words or in slang words which put a challenge to generate right patterns. Currently there is no mechanism to deal with this type of issue is carried out. The future researchers can work on this to generate more accurate patterns.

CPSIA information can be obtained
at www.ICGtesting.com
Printed in the USA
LVHW020014280423
745413LV00009B/242